# Opened Windows

by
James Alexander Stewart

Foreword by the Rev. W. P. Nicholson

First Published 1958

Copyright
ISBN 1-56632-059-3

Printed in the United States of America.

This book is sincerely dedicated to a
mother in Israel
MRS. ANGHEL TCHIVIDJIAN
whose constant intercession for
worldwide revival
has greatly inspired the author

Bring ye all the tithes into the storehouse, that there may be meat in mine house, and prove me now herewith, saith the LORD of hosts, if I will not open you the windows of heaven, and pour you out a blessing, that there shall not be room enough to receive it.

—Malachi 3:10

# Foreword

I have known Rev. James Stewart for many years. I have followed his life and work with increased interest. He has been, and is still, "a vessel unto honour, sanctified, and meet for the Master's use, and prepared unto every good work." Through European countries he has brought thousands to Christ by his preaching and teaching. He has been used of God to promote revivals in many places where he has labored.

His book *Opened Windows* contains the methods and messages used by him to do this sort of work. He knows from a long and wide and successful experience what a revival is. His book *Opened Windows* gives clear and scriptural instructions on how to prepare for a revival, as well as pay the price of it. Some can and do write fluently about revivals, sometimes in favor of them, sometimes against them, but they are merely writing about something they have never seen as fact. All their knowledge is acquired from what they have read or heard. Here is a book filled with instructions that have been hammered out on the anvil of experience. It is written so sublimely simple, and so scriptural, and easily understood, the wayfaring man need not err therein. I trust it may have a very wide circulation, and be greatly used of God to stimulate desire in the hearts of ministers and Christian workers for a revival. *Opened Windows* will guide and direct them, and save

7

them from mistakes and errors. I sincerely wish it every success and God's richest blessing on it.

—W. P. Nicholson

# Contents

# Introduction

As we approach this sacred theme of revival we remember the words of Andrew Murray when led to write on the Holy Spirit. "I will meditate and be still," he wrote, "until something of the overwhelming truth of the theme falls on me, and faith begins to realize it."

It is with hesitancy and awe that this writer approaches his subject because of the wonder of the experience. I have been astonished in reading over the history of revivals to see how few of the chosen instruments whom the Lord mightily used have recorded anything of their experience. Could the reason be that the theme was too sacred? Could it be that those who were best qualified to write were simply overwhelmed with the glory of it? It may be they felt like Thomas John of Wales, when God worked wondrously at the annual convocation of the Calvinist Methodist Church in August, 1859. Thomas John was found alone in a field after the service, lost in wonder. A friend approached him and said, "Brother John, was not the sight of the thousands as they prayed silently a most impressive one? Did you ever see anything to compare with it?"

"I never saw one of them," was the answer. "I saw no one but God!"

In Revelation, chapter one, we have an account of a personal revival experience in the life of John the Beloved, on the lonely Isle of Patmos. Having been banished for the sake of the "Word of God and the testimony of Jesus Christ," he desperately needed a fresh vision of his wondrous Lord. Upon hearing a voice, like the sound of a trumpet, he turned and saw his Redeemer in all His matchless beauty and glory, as the kingly High Priest of the Church. The apostle, when speaking later of this experience, says: "And when I saw him, I fell at His feet as dead" (Rev. 1:17).

Because of the sacredness and glory of the experience of revival it is not easy to speak on this subject to any group of Christian workers unless they have been prepared by the Spirit to receive the message. I am reminded of an experience I had once when crossing the Atlantic. Sharing the cabin with me was a diamond merchant from Amsterdam, who was on his way to New York to sell precious stones. Upon my request, he showed me a few samples he had with him. Later, he confessed to me that he had some of far greater beauty and value locked away. "I am sorry," he explained, "I would like to show you those stones also, but it is only on very rare occasions that I ever show them, since there are so few people who have a proper appreciation for stones of such worth."

Even Jonathan Edwards, one of the greatest intellects of all times, had great difficulty in describing the mighty workings of the Holy Spirit in *The Great Awakening*. One of the reasons why it is difficult to speak to Christian workers today on this subject is that the majority of evangelicals are only interested in the phase of revival which appeals outwardly to the carnal mind. This was true even during the Welsh revival of 1904. Seth Joshua, who was used of God in that movement, stated years later: "The Welsh revival was the product of much soul agony. In its initial stages the production retained its full bloom, as when a peach is plucked from a tree. It lost this quality when human fingers played with it, and newspapers reported every odd thing for the sake of circulation among the people who desired the human side made public. Reports threw light on the human side of things and the divine was forgotten."

I thus beg the reader to approach the contents of this book with unsandalled feet. There is nothing sensational here for the unsanctified mind. This book is written for those believers who are desperate, for those who have been brought low before the Lord and who are now crying in the secret place, "O Lord, revive Thy work!" (Hab. 3:2).

Many friends have found great blessing on reading our books, a portion at a time, at family worship or at prayer meetings.

This book is sent forth with a fervent prayer that the Head of the Church will be pleased to use it in the preparation of the saints for worldwide revival. The greatest need of the hour is for a band of born-again believers in every village, city, county and country, initiated into the mysteries of the workings of the Spirit, to labor for, and labor in, the coming revival. May God grant this for His glory. "Behold, the days come, saith the Lord, that the plowman shall overtake the reaper, and the treader of grapes him that soweth seed; and the mountains shall drop sweet wine, and all the hills shall melt" (Amos 9:13).

# I

# Evangelism and Revival

"Revival includes evangelism, but evangelism may not include revival. Evangelism always follows revival, but revival does not necessarily follow an evangelistic campaign.

"Evangelism seeks the evangelism of sinners who are dead in sin; revival is a spiritual quickening of the life of the redeemed."

—J.A.S.

The majority of Christians today confuse revival with the work of evangelism. Such confusion is easy to understand, since revival results in a great wave of evangelism and ingathering of souls. Revival includes evangelism, but evangelism may not include revival. Evangelism always follows revival, but revival does not necessarily follow an evangelistic campaign.

Evangelism seeks the resurrection of sinners who are dead in trespasses and sin. Revival is a spiritual quickening of the life of the redeemed. The aim of evangelism is to reach out after the lost souls, while that of revival is to bring new life and vitality to the saints of God through a renewal of the presence and power of the Holy Spirit. Revival means a fresh incoming of the Divine Life into a body threatening to become a corpse.

*Only on rare occasions does spontaneous revival spring from organized evangelism.* The mighty movements of the Holy Ghost in the ministry of D. L. Moody, R. A. Torrey, Wilbur Chapman, A. C. Dixon, and other such spiritual giants are some of the rare occasions. The promotion and preparation of evangelism and revival is approached from different angles. For an evangelistic campaign one plans and organizes through several committees, thus preparing the way for the arrival of an evangelistic party in which the chief evangelist is the center of attraction. Consequently, when the campaign is finished, the attendance and the enthusiasm of the

17

crowds subside, since the center of attraction has gone. Because of the great amount of publicity, the Christians talk a great deal about the evangelistic party, so that it is only natural that when the party leaves the scene, and the publicity is finished, the people more or less lose interest. If the so-called "revival" is the result of great organization and advertising alone, then in order to maintain the interest there must be a continuation of the organization on an even greater scale after the meetings have finished. On the other hand, on those rare occasions when spontaneous revival breaks out from an organized effort, the interest of the crowds, as well as the Lord's blessing, is greater after the campaign has closed. In fact, the numbers in attendance at meetings are increased and the blessing attending the Word is deeper and fuller than ever. Sometimes the blessing goes on in an even greater way for months and even years after the campaign. The Spirit breaks through all programs and organizations as He holds full sway in the Church. I have never known a revival that did not disorganize man's plans and blueprints.

With revival in view, the Church plans and prepares for the advent of the Holy Spirit in their midst, where the living Lord Jesus will be the center of attraction, as recorded in Mark 2:1: "And it was noised that *He* was in the house." The acid test of all true revivals is the powerful presence of the majestic Christ known and felt in all His beauty and glory. Thus thousands of saints are drawn together *for no other reason* than that He is in the midst (Rev. 1:9-18).

What a textbook on revival is the study of the Spirit's work in 1904 in the Principality of Wales. It is true that God mightily used R. B. Jones, Seth Joshua, George Clark, Sydney Evans, and Evan Roberts, but the revival fires were independent of them. Hundreds of preachers took part, while in many places the fire burned greatest where there were no great

18

preachers. In fact, there was little ministry at that time for such well-known figures as Campbell Morgan, Gypsy Smith, and others of like caliber. These dear men of God came reverently to the revival country and took their shoes from off their feet as they stood on holy ground. In the later stages of the revival Evan Roberts was the well-known figurehead, but that was the result of newspaper publicity. The true spiritual saints knew that the Holy Ghost was the instigator of the movement and the Son of God the center of attraction. This fact was brought home to me recently as I sat in the home where Mr. Roberts was born and where he prayed through, and I heard in hushed tones an account of that mighty movement from his sister and brother-in-law. (It seemed as if I, myself, were living through those mighty days. The heavens were opened and the sense of the Lord's presence was overwhelming.) God's servants recounted how thousands of people gathered in many places all over the nation apart from the presence of Evan Roberts. In fact, it was rarely announced where or when he would speak. The people had gathered because the risen, ascended Redeemer was in their midst.

*Another distinguishing feature* of *revival is its spontaneity. It is a movement that cannot be arranged as in a series of special meetings.* The true spirit of revival eludes the grasp of the organizer and the advertiser. It cannot be created by machinery nor promoted by printer's ink. The two symbols of Pentecost were wind and fire. Both of these speak to us of the mystical, supernatural, sovereign work of the Holy Spirit in revival. One cannot organize a cyclone or predict the course of a prairie fire. John Shearer of Scotland writes: "A great revival is like a forest fire; you may trace its early course, following the first lines of flame, but soon its progress is so swift and widely diffused that the eye can no longer keep pace with it. The flames burst forth at once in many places, and now we see but one great conflagration." In John 3:8 the Saviour expounds the mysterious, supernatural, spontaneous ministry of the Holy Spirit in simple and definite terms: "The wind bloweth where it listeth, and thou hearest the sound thereof, but canst not tell whence it cometh, and whither it goeth." So it is in days of revival. This truth was demonstrated during those blessed days of 1860 and around that period in the northeast of Scotland where spiritual fires were burning simultaneously in many places apart from all planned evangelistic campaigns. At that time Duncan Matheson, Reginald Ratcliffe, and James Turner went from village to village and from town to town reaping a mighty harvest of souls whose hearts were prepared by the Spirit.

It is a revelation to one who has studied minutely the revival ministry of William C. Burns in Scotland to see how the movement there was so free and spontaneous. As the Spirit of God guided him he went from town to town, sometimes remaining three days, sometimes three months. No set time was fixed for the duration of the meetings. It was simply announced that Mr. Burns was coming for three or four evenings to minister, and that he would carry on as the Lord blessed the Word. Often thousands would gather without any announcement at all for an extra meeting, so that the young servant had to be called. On other occasions many hundreds would follow him late at night to the home where he was living, in deep distress of soul, that he might preach once again the glorious Gospel of God's grace in forgiveness.

Many times in Europe we have known large numbers to gather in the early morning hour for prayer without any public announcement being given. They were drawn together in a certain place only by the compulsion of the Spirit. They were pleasantly surprised to see others there, as they thought that they would be alone at the place.

*It is striking to notice in the mightiest work of the* Spirit *ever known on the North American continent that the revival broke out in the ordinary ministry of a faithful pastor.* No special evangelistic campaign was in progress. No outside visiting speaker was featured. Jonathan Edwards and his people had been deeply concerned about the spiritual condition of Northampton in New England. This prophet of the Great Awakening kept on preaching the Word in a faithful manner. Then, suddenly without any warning, the Holy Spirit came in such mighty power that the spiritual face of America was changed. In his spiritual classic, *The Narrative,* Edwards describes the sudden awakening in the following words:

"Presently upon this, a great and earnest concern about the great things of religion, and the eternal world, became universal in all parts of the town, and among persons of all degrees and all ages; the noise among the dry bones waxed louder and louder; all other talk but about spiritual and eternal things was soon thrown by; all the conversations in all companies and upon all occasions were upon these things only, unless so much as was necessary for people carrying on their ordinary secular business. Other discourse than on the things of religion would scarcely be tolerated in any company. . . . Religion was with all sorts the great concern, and the world was only a thing by-the-by. The only thing in their view was to get into the kingdom of heaven, and everyone appeared to be pressing into it. . . . There was scarcely a person in the town either old or young that was left unconcerned about the great things of the eternal world. Those that were wont to be vainest and loosest, and those that had been most disposed to think and speak slightly of vital and experimental religion, were now subject to great awakenings. And the work of conversion was carried on in a most astonishing manner, and increased more and more. Souls did, as it were, come by flocks to Jesus Christ. . . . This work of God, as it was carried on and the number of true saints multiplied, soon made a glorious alteration in the town; so that in the spring and summer following 1735 the town seemed to be full of the presence of God: it never was so full of love, nor so full of joy; and yet so full of distress, as it was then. There were remarkable tokens of God's presence in almost every house. It was a time of joy and calmness on account of salvation's having been brought into them; parents rejoicing over their children as newborn, and husbands over their wives, and wives over their husbands. The goings of God were then seen in the sanctuary; God's day was a delight and His tabernacles were amiable. Our public assemblies were then beautiful; the congregation was alive in God's service, everyone earnestly intent on the public worship. Every hearer was eager to drink in the words of the minister as they came from his mouth; the assembly in general was from time to time in tears as the Word was preached; some weeping with sorrow and distress, others with joy and love, others with pity and concern for the souls of their neighbor."

*I would pause here to make it clear that, as an evangelist myself, I would in no way discredit the work of organized evangelism.* So great importance do I place upon the work of an evangelist that, if I were a pastor, I should seek to invite an evangelist for a campaign in my church for at least a month twice a year. A church which ceases to evangelize will soon cease to be evangelical. A church which does not evangelize will fossilize! Evangelism is the chief business of the Church. Personal soul winning has its place but it cannot take the place of a united evangelistic effort. When I was a boy, just starting to preach, I was warned by my spiritual father, Mr. Tom Rea of Belfast, that if any assembly or group of believers invited me for an evangelistic effort for less than one month, then I should conclude that they were not in earnest! I thank God for all the glorious healthy campaigns being carried on today through every evangelist. As one of the gifts of our ascended Lord to the Church, the evangelist should be heartily received and supported. Spirit-filled evangelists are desperately needed today. Spirit-filled believers likewise are desperately needed today to sponsor the evangelists in their God-given ministry.

As a boy evangelist, however, I soon learned that my labors in evangelism were greatly hindered by the low spiritual condition of the Lord's people. Nothing breaks the heart of an evangelist so quickly as to see and feel the deadness in the group with whom he comes to labor. Every true evangelist knows the grief and strain of trying to preach the Gospel to the unsaved and to win souls for Christ in an assembly of God's people who are cold and indifferent. How many times I, myself, could not sleep, eat or even preach because of the awful apathy and unconcern of the saints. I have been puzzled again and again as to why I was invited by these people for an evangelistic effort in the first place. Dr. Hyman Appelman speaks for all of us when he says: "When I come for a meeting, and on the first night, and the second night, and the third night, the prayer rooms are full, I know in my heart that there are not enough demons in hell to keep us from revival blessing. But oh, when I come to a place—to have to pull, to have to beg, to have to plead, to have to scold, to have to agonize, to have to abuse, to have to whip, to have to scourge, in order to get people to pray—that is when my heart breaks; that is when the load becomes fearfully heavy."

*On the other hand, how easy it is to evangelize in the atmosphere of revival!* One can preach five times daily for several months without feeling the strain of weariness. Many young evangelists are astonished when they read of the strenuous labors of John Wesley, who covered the British Isles on

23

horseback year after year, preaching from five o'clock in the morning till near midnight, day after day, to a ripe old age. The explanation is simple: he was evangelizing during a time of deep spiritual awakening in the Church. The standard of holiness among the saints had been raised high by John and his brother Charles and their associates.

I have found during my long experience in evangelism that if I can stay in a place long enough to lead God's people into a state of revival, the task of preaching the Gospel is reduced to simply explaining the way of salvation and giving the invitation to seeking, burdened souls. When the saints are revived each becomes burdened about the lost about him— his loved ones, his neighbor, his business companions, and all whom he knows. Prayer meetings are crowded with everyone wanting to make requests for prayer for the salvation of his loved ones. At each prayer hour the leader of the meeting finds great stacks of papers on which are written the prayer burdens of the redeemed. Sometimes it takes half an hour just to read out the requests: Pray for my son . . . for my daughter . . . for my husband . . . for my neighbor. Each prayer meeting is one groan in the Spirit for lost souls, as each seeks to bear the burden of the other in his longing after his loved ones. In such meetings there is a desperateness about the requests and the prayers, mingled with confidence that God answers prayer. Such confidence produces an expectancy in the meetings which is felt in the very atmosphere. With each believer working for, praying for, believing for the salvation of his own lost ones, it is little wonder that great conviction comes upon the unsaved in the meetings. It is little wonder that there is a stir among the godless in the town or city. It is inevitable that souls should be saved during such times! With what joy the believers and the evangelist work together to gather in the harvest of lost souls! Such an experience is fervently described in the favorite hymn of the '59 revival in Ulster when, in revival meetings, in the streets, on the wayside, in the factories, in the fields and in the homes the people sang joyfully:

*Whene'er we meet, you always say,*
    *What's the news? What's the news?*
*Pray what's the order of the day?*
    *What's the news? What's the news?*
*Oh, I have got good news to tell:*
    *My Saviour has done all things well,*
*And triumph'd over death and hell;*
    *That's the news! That's the news!*

*The Lamb was slain on Calvary—*
    *That's the news! That's the news!*
*To set a world of sinners free—*
    *That's the news! That's the news!*
*'Twas there His precious blood was shed;*
    *'Twas there he bowed His sacred head;*
*But now He's risen from the dead—*
    *That's the news! That's the news!*

*His work's reviving all around—*
    *That's the news! That's the news!*
*And many have salvation found—*
    *That's the news! That's the news!*
*And since their souls have caught the flame,*
    *They shout Hosannah to His name,*
*And all around they spread His fame—*
    *That's the news! That's the news!*

*The Lord has pardoned all my sins—*
    *That's the news! That's the news!*
*I have the witness now within—*

*That's the news! That's the news!*
*And since He took my sins away,*
*    And taught me how to watch and pray,*
*I'm happy now from day to day—*
*    That's the news! That's the news!*

*And Christ the Lord can save you now—*
*    That's the news! That's the news!*
*Your sinful heart He can renew—*
*    That's the news! That's the news!*
*This moment, if for sins you grieve—*
*    This moment, if you do believe—*
*A full acquittal you'll receive—*
*    That's the news! That's the news!*

*And then, if anyone should say,*
*    What's the news? What's the news?*
*Oh! tell them you've begun to pray—*
*    That's the news! That's the news!*
*That you have joined the conquering band,*
*    And now with joy at God's command,*
*You're marching to the Better Land—*
*    That's the news! That's the news!*

# II

## The Subnormal Church
## and Revival

"A church that needs to be revived is a church that is living below the norm of the New Testament pattern."

"So low has become the spiritual life of the average believer, that the glorious state which revival brings would seem abnormal to him."

—J.A.S.

Mr. D. M. McIntyre has told of a glorious church edifice in Florence which came fresh from the hands of builders and artists about the middle of the fifteenth century. Its severe outlines were relieved by delicate tinting on roof and walls; its choir and chapels were lit up with priceless examples of mural decorations. A century passed, and then Giorgio Vasari broke in upon the scheme of the decoration by the erection of his hideous stone altars. Some of the frescoes were obliterated, others were mutilated. Those which remained were buried under a coating of whitewash. To hide the vandalism, it was judged necessary to whiten the walls also, and the deep roof, while the spring of the arches was painted in a dull ochre. Then, that the glare of light might be reduced, nineteen large windows were built up. And so, obscured and dishonored, the great church building stood during three hundred years. It was known by the Florentines that the coarse distemper hid the superb frescoes of the Giotto Agnolo Gaddi and Maso di Banco, but no one was able to say how the covering might be removed without destroying the exquisite harmonies underneath. At last, some hundred years ago, a way was found and tried—costly and tedious—but practical. And now, in various portions, the church edifice begins to shine out in almost its pristine splendor. The work progresses slowly; there is still much to do, but one may at least trace the design of the builder and the motive of the artist.

The Church of Jesus Christ came in its pure glory, unsullied from the hand of its Divine Artificer, but all too soon its splendor was darkened and its beauty stained. Yet, there have been times of refreshing from the Lord in which the intrusive unsightliness has been in part cleared away. And at such times one begins anew to realize what the Church of the Firstborn in the days of its inception must have been.

John Wesley gives us a glimpse into a church which had been so restored to apostolic devotion, purity, and power. Writing of his visit among the Moravians, he says, "God has given me at length the desire of my heart. I am with a church whose conversation is in Heaven, in whom is the mind that was in Christ, and who so walk as He walked. Here I continually meet what I sought for—living proofs of the power of faith, persons saved from inward, as well as outward sin, by the love of God shed abroad in their hearts. I am extremely comforted and strengthened by the conversation of this lovely people."

*The tragedy in the history of the Pilgrim Church on earth is that generation after generation has lived and died without even a faint glimpse of that splendor which shines through during such times of refreshing and restoration.* The purpose of God in redemption—i.e. "That he might present it to himself a glorious church, not having spot, or wrinkle, or any such thing; but that it should be holy and without blemish" (Eph. 5:27)—has been dimmed or entirely hidden away under the stains of worldliness and carnality. *Thus there has been constant need for revival in her midst.*

One feels that just here it is necessary to rediscover the true meaning of the word "revival." This word has been so used with varying connotations that it has lost its original meaning. That which the average child of God calls revival is not revival at all in the true scriptural sense of the word. Too often the word has been associated with showmanship, sensationalism, and commercialism.

There are some who even hesitate to use the word because it represents that which seems to lack reverence, humility, and permanence. Actually today any series of meetings is termed revival. I plead with my brethren to rescue this sacred word for use in its original meaning. If revival is the need of the hour, then we must agree on what revival is. If every series of meetings can be called by this name, then how will the Lord's people be able to pray in unity and seek intelligently for the real revival?

*In the revivals under Hezekiah, Josiah, and Nehemiah we see that the work was one* of *recovery and restoration.* The spiritual life of the nation had sunk low; the people had departed from the commandments of the Lord and thus were living in disobedience. It was when these men of God read the Holy Scriptures once again and saw God's plan and purpose for His people, that they called the people to repentance and sought a recovery. It was a revival of the reading of the Word of God and a revival of the obeying of the Word of God. It was the Word applied by the mighty power of the Holy Ghost that wrought repentance and brought the backslidden nation back to God's original pattern of worship and service, as given to Moses on the mount. The predominant meaning of the word "revival" in the Old Testament is to recover, "to restore," "to return" to God's original standard for His people.

The Greek word for revival is ANAZOPUREO, which means "to stir up or rekindle a fire which is slowly dying," "to keep in full flame." It is used metaphorically in 2 Timothy 1:6, when Paul says to Timothy, "Wherefore I put thee in remembrance that thou stir up the gift of God, which is in thee. . . ." Don't let it die out; kindle it afresh and keep it in full flame!

Another related word, ANATHALLO, is translated "flourish" in Philippians 4:10: "Your care of me hath flourished again." The literal meaning of the word is "to put forth fresh shoots." The picture here is that of the coming of spring bringing new life to trees and vegetation, as described in Song of Solomon 2:11-13: "For, lo, the winter is past, the rain is over and gone; the flowers appear on the earth; the time of the singing of birds is come, and the voice of the turtle is heard in our land; the fig tree putteth forth her green figs, and the vines with the tender grape give a good smell." "They that dwell under His shadow shall return; they shall revive as the corn, and grow as the vine" (Hos. 14:7).

The word used for "revival" in many of our European Bibles is the word "awakening," so that when believers on the Continent pray for revival they are actually praying for an awakening and a quickening among the sleeping, careless, backslidden Christians.

*The term "revival" presupposes a deterioration and declension, a falling away, a slackening of the reins.* A church that needs to be revived is a church that is living below the norm of the New Testament pattern. Its members, who need to be quickened, are living a subnormal Christian life. The fire of devotion to Christ and the fire of zeal for lost souls is slowly dying, and needs to be rekindled. It is a tragic fact that the vast majority of Christians today are living a subnormal Christian life. So low has become the spiritual life of the average believer that the glorious state which revival brings would seem abnormal to him. We have come to regard the low state of our experience in the Church as normal and the blessed reviving of the Spirit as extraordinary or abnormal.

Coldness, callousness, deadness, and backslidings are abnormal, and the Church will never become normal until she sees revival. *The glorious splendor of the church which shines out as the result of revival is the true standard our Lord has set up in the New Testament, and this is what He expects to see among His redeemed ones at all times.* There is nothing abnormal about the revived Church of God. The only thing abnormal about the Church today is that she *needs* to be revived. There is nothing abnormal about being filled with the Spirit, according to Ephesians 5:18. There is nothing abnormal about sanctifying Christ in the heart, as we are commanded in 1 Peter 3:15. There is nothing abnormal in a Christian's "reign in life by one, Jesus Christ," as mentioned in Romans 5:17. There is nothing abnormal in a redeemed child of God presenting his body a living sacrifice, as Paul adjures us to do in Romans 12:1. There is nothing abnormal in receiving a mighty baptism of power for winning lost souls to Christ. These things represent the normal Christian life as set forth for us in the New Testament. Adolf Monod, when dying, gasped out four telling utterances: "All in Christ—By the Holy Spirit—For the glory of God—All else is nothing!"

The false thinking concerning revival may be attributed to the erroneous teaching of the past years, that the acceptance of the Lordship of Christ is a second experience of grace which is a sort of optional addendum to the Christian life. The Spirit-filled life has been set forth as a spiritual luxury which is only for a few Christian aristocrats—something fine and noble, but not a necessary demand upon every redeemed child of God. Consequently we have such terms as "the higher life," "the deeper life," "the victorious Christian life," specifying a quality of spiritual life which is abnormal, extraordinary, and practically unattainable for the average Christian. Many have come to me at Bible conferences, after I have

33

pressed home the absolute necessity of living habitually the spiritual life which is set forth in the New Testament, and have said, even weeping, "Mr. Stewart, we have been saved for many years, and have always thought that the norm for the Christian life was that of defeat and failure while we walk this earth. We never knew that such a life as you describe is not only possible, but it is *God's standard of* holiness for every one of His children."

In the early days of the Church in Uganda, a boy who had been baptized came to Mr. Pilkington and told him of his failure to be true to Christ in the pathetic words: "I sin as much as I ever did." The mighty man of God was cut to the quick, and the desire for fresh spiritual power was deepened in his heart. Shortly afterwards, he went apart onto one of the islands in Victoria Nyanza, that he might wait upon God and receive fresh power from Him. His prayers were answered, and later he could write to Bishop Tucker, "I want to tell you that we are in the midst of a time of great blessing. God has enabled several of us to see that for a long time past we have been working in our own strength, and that consequently there has been no power in our lives, and very little blessing. *We have, however, been brought to see that the command, 'Be filled with the Spirit,' is as much laid upon us as upon the Ephesians, and that power for effectual service is placed at our disposal if we will appropriate it.* I cannot tell you the difference it has made to us in our lives, as well as in our work. We are full of joy, whereas a little while ago the depression was almost unbearable. As for our work, God is now using us, and a wonderful wave of blessing is passing over the land." Thus began one of the mightiest movements of the Spirit in the annals of foreign mission activity.

*We must be very careful to differentiate between revival in itself, and the spiritual state resulting from revival.*

34

*REVIVAL is not God's standard for the Church but is the process through which the Church is restored to its former splendor and glory:* "Wilt thou not revive us again: that thy people may rejoice in thee?" (Ps. 85:6). In days of revival there is a great time of heart-searching, when believers are smitten by the Holy Spirit as they realize afresh how far they have departed from the Lord. This spirit of brokenness results in deep humiliation, repentance, confession and restitution. The pathway of humiliation is only the gateway to our receiving all God's fullness in His beloved Son. It is not enough to be emptied and broken down before the Lord—the believer must be filled. In order to be filled with all the fullness of God, and to live the normal, healthy, dynamic Christian life, the stricken believer must appropriate the risen, reigning life of Christ for his practical *daily walk.* "That the God of our Lord Jesus Christ, the Father of glory, may give unto you the spirit of wisdom and revelation in the knowledge of him: The eyes of your understanding being enlightened; that ye may know what is the hope of his calling, and what the riches of the glory of his inheritance in the saints, And what is the exceeding greatness of his power to us-ward who believe, according to the working of his mighty power, Which he wrought in Christ, when he raised him from the dead, and set him at his own right hand in the heavenly places, Far above all principality, and power, and might, and dominion, and every name that is named, not only in this world, but also in that which is to come: And hath put all things under his feet, and gave him to be the head over all things to the church, Which is his body, the fulness of him that filleth all in all. . . . But God, who is rich in mercy, for his great love wherewith he loved us . . . And hath raised us up together, and made us sit together in heavenly places in Christ Jesus" (Eph. 1:17-23; 2:4,6).

I was preaching a Bible conference in North America once when God began to move among His people—so much so that I could not continue preaching as there was such an outburst of confession among the convicted ones which continued for several hours. Some spiritual leaders present were praising the Lord that revival had now come. Had they not been praying for revival for many years? And now this was the answer to their earnest supplications. Somehow, though, I could not enter into their rejoicing as the saints of God continued their confessions before the Lord. I was deeply disturbed and broken myself to think of the lying, gossiping, stealing, cheating, the hatred, the impure thoughts, the coldness, the indifference, that had characterized their lives. I explained to the leaders that it was disturbing to me that such confessions were *necessary* among God's people and that certainly the heart of our Heavenly Father must be broken at this low state of spirituality.

The joy which came from seeing God work was overshadowed by the realization that God's children had been living such lives of defeat and dishonor. I further explained to my brethren that while we were indeed in a process of revival, this is not God's norm for His people. *This spirit of brokenness and repentance in sackcloth and ashes must now be followed by a definite act of deliverance from defeat and failure and a renewed life of holiness and power.*

When I first began my ministry as an evangelist I had little time for Bible conferences or conventions for the deepening of spiritual life, as I felt that this was a waste of my time when I should be out winning souls for Christ. I even went so far as to argue with Christian leaders that the Church would better serve the Lord's purpose by having more evangelistic campaigns rather than this type of ministry. I argued further that holiness conventions never produced revival. I was not very long living in this state, however, before the Word of God and experience taught me that the work of soul-winning is hard and difficult until there is a higher standard of holiness in the Church. While ministering a few years ago at the Welsh Keswick Convention, I learned first hand that it was the presentation by Dr. F. B. Meyer of God's standard of holiness that laid the foundation for the revival in that country in 1904. A few pastors, burdened before the Lord concerning the desperate need of their own churches to return to vital New Testament Christianity, sent for God's servant to come and minister to them. The Spirit of the Lord rested mightily upon him as he showed from the Word what God expected of His people. These preachers went back to their congregations to raise the standard of scriptural holiness among their people. Very soon, the fire of God began to break out simultaneously in different parts of the country until the whole nation was aflame.

"Who brought the revival to you?" was the question once asked of an old minister during times of refreshing from the Lord in Wales.

"No one," he replied; "we got revived."

Oh that God would burden us all with a passion to see His Church brought out of, and lifted up above, her present subnormal condition!

> O Breath of Life, come sweeping through us,
>     Revive Thy Church with life and power;
> O Breath of Life, come, cleanse, renew us
>     And fit Thy Church to meet this hour.
>
> O Wind of God, come bend us, break us,
>     Till humbly we confess our need;
> Then in Thy tenderness remake us,
>     Revive, restore, for this we plead.

# III

# The Normal Christian and Revival

"We believe there are many sincere Christians who are living defeated lives because they are not aware of the full provision which is theirs in Christ."

—J.A.S.

Mr. A. J. Gordon has rightly said, "When I hear Christians testify that they would be satisfied with the lowest place in heaven if only by the grace of God they are permitted to reach there at all, I reply that their Lord will not be so easily satisfied if they are. He wants them to strive for the highest place, for a seat nearest the Throne, and for a crown of the brightest luster. We must look out that our humility is not indolence with a solemn countenance upon it, the real fact being that we are content with the lowest place in heaven because we have not energy and self-sacrifice enough to make us strive after the highest."

Many a Christian's experience is not the true Christian experience. How many a believer has often said in the secret place before God:

> Sometimes I catch sweet glimpses of His face,
> But that is all.
> Sometimes He looks on me and seems to smile,
> But that is all.
> Sometimes He speaks a passing word of peace,
> But that is all.
> Sometimes I think I hear His loving voice
> Upon me call.
> And is this all He meant when thus He Spoke—
> "Come unto Me!"?

—Horatius Bonar

No, beloved friend, this is not all. There is a deeper more enduring life of constant fellowship and holiness in Him. Bishop Handley Moule, to my mind, has given us the finest description of the normal Christian which can be found in the English language:

"It is nothing less than the supreme aim of the Christian Gospel that we should be holy; that the God of Peace should sanctify us through and through our being; that we should walk worthy of the Lord unto all pleasing ('all studious meeting of His Will', as the Greek of Col. 1:9-10 imports). It is the insatiable desire of the soul, which has truly seen the Lord, to be made fully like Him by His grace.

"Of our aims, how shall I speak both briefly enough and greatly enough? They are just this—to be like Him, 'whom not having seen we love;' to displace accordingly, in grave reality, self from the inner throne, and to enthrone Him; to make not the slightest compromise with the smallest sin. We aim at being entirely willing, nay, definitely to will, to know with ever keener sensibility what is sin in us, and where it is, that it may be dealt with at once by the Holy Spirit. We aim at nothing less than to walk with God all day long; to abide every hour in Christ, and He and His words in us; to love God with all the heart, and our neighbor as ourselves; to live, and that in no conventional sense, 'no longer to ourselves, but to Him who died for us, and rose again.' We aim at 'yielding ourselves to God' as the unregenerate will yields itself to sin, to self; at having every thought brought into captivity to the obedience of Christ—every thought, every movement of the inner world; a strict comprehensive captivity and absolute and arbitrary slavery.

"In the region of outward life our aim is, of course, equally large and pervading. It is to break with all evil, and follow all good. It is never, never more to speak evil of any man; never

42

to lose patience; never to trifle with wrong: whether impurity, untruth, or unkindness; never in any known thing to evade our Master's will; never to be ashamed of His Name. I emphasize again and again this *never,* for there is the point. As believers in our Lord Jesus Christ, as those who are not their own, but bought, and who accordingly, in the strictest sense, belong to Him all through, our aim is, it must be, across any amount of counterthoughts, *'never to grieve Him, never to stray; always in the inner world, always in the outer, to walk and to please Him.'* I say again, this is our aim, not in any conventional sense, such as to leave us easy and tolerably comfortable when we fail. Not so; God forbid. Failure, when it comes across this aim, will come with a pang of shame and disappointment, which we shall little wish to feel again. It will be a deeply conscious discord and collision. It will be a fall down a rough steep. It will be a joy lost, or at best deferred again. It will be the missing of a divine smile, the loss of the light of the countenance of the King.

"It is possible, I dare to say, for those who will indeed draw on their Lord's power for deliverance and power, to live a life—how shall I describe it?—a life in which His promises are taken as they stand, and found to be true. It is possible to cast every care on Him daily, and to be at peace amidst the pressure. It is possible to have affections and imaginations purified through faith, in a profound and practical sense. It is possible to see the will of God in everything and to find it, as one has said, no longer a sigh, but a song. It is possible, in the world of inner act and motion, to put away, to cause to be put away, all bitterness, and wrath, and anger and evil speaking, daily and hourly. It is possible, by unreserved resort to divine power, under divine conditions, to become strongest, through and through, at our weakest point, to find the thing which yesterday upset all our obligations to patience,

43

or to purity, or to humility, an occasion today, through Him who loveth us and worketh in us, for a joyful consent to His will, and a delightful sense of His presence and sin-annulling power. *These are things divinely possible, and because they are His work, the genuine experience of them will lay us, must lay us, only lower at His feet, and leave us only more athirst for more!"*

*It is not only possible,* but it is the will of God that every redeemed soul should attain to and maintain such a standard of Christian living throughout his entire life, from the day of his salvation to the day of his translation. This is the message of the church epistles of the New Testament. Three-fourths of the teachings of these epistles concerns the practical holy walk of the believer here on earth. Salvation is set forth in these epistles in three tenses: salvation begun, salvation continuing, and salvation consummated.

We all love the delightful story told of a great Greek scholar. One day he was listening intently in the open air to the Salvation Army as they gave forth God's glorious message of salvation. He was suddenly accosted by a young Salvation Army lassie, who asked the clergyman with deep earnestness, "Sir, are you saved?" The old gentleman looked down with a beautiful smile and said to her, "Do you mean ESOTHEN or do you mean SOZOMINOS? Or do you mean SOTHESOMAI?" She looked up with wonder and asked the Bishop whatever he was talking about. "Sir;"she persisted, "I want to know are you saved from hell?" He later explained to her that he was asking if she meant, "Have I been saved?" or, "Am I being saved?" or, did she mean, "Will I be saved?"

*It is the present tense of the Gospel, that is, "being saved," that is dealt with most in the Scriptures.* For example, in Romans 5:10, we read, "For if, when we were enemies, we were reconciled to God by the death of his son, much more, being reconciled, we shall be saved by his life." The believer is saved from the power of sin day by day by the ascension-life of the Lord Jesus. "Wherefore he is able also to save them to the uttermost that come unto God by him, seeing he ever liveth to make intercession for them" (Heb. 7:25). He is able to save us completely because of this high-priestly ministry. This is the glorious *unfinished* work of Christ.

The good news of the present tense of the Gospel to the believer is that God has made ample provision for the dynamic life which He intends us to live. In the "Alps of the New Testament" the Apostle Paul soars into the dizzy heights of the believer's resources. After saluting the saints at Ephesus, the apostle plunges into his glorious theme of the believer's potential riches. He is impatient to proclaim to them their wealth in Christ Jesus. He begins with a doxology: "Blessed be the God and Father of our Lord Jesus Christ, who hath blessed us with all spiritual blessings in heavenly places in Christ" (1:3). In verse 6 he tells them that they have been highly graced in the Beloved One. This verse leads them to the gateway of the glorious deposits which are theirs: "To the praise of the glory of his grace, wherein he hath made us accepted in the beloved." As we scan our title deeds we discover that the word "riches" is the key word throughout this epistle. In chapter 2, verse 7, we read, ". . . the exceeding riches of his grace." The word translated "exceeding" is that from which we get our English Word "hyperbole," applied to exaggeration. The word literally means, "to shoot beyond the mark" and implies therefore the thought of excess. Paul means that although one uses the utmost wealth of language in speaking of these riches, he cannot shoot beyond the mark; the riches of God exceed all power of expression. Again in chapter 3, verse 8, the apostle speaks of the "unsearchable riches of Christ." The word "unsearchable" means "riches that can never be explored." We not only cannot measure them, and we not only can form no estimate of them, but we can never get to the end of our exploration. There is a boundless continent of riches that still lies before us, when we have carried our search to the limit. Here our spiritual Geiger-counters are helpless in exploring all the riches which are potentially ours in Christ. Not only so, but these riches are *"untraceable."* The thought is that of seeking to trace a path through the woods, and finding so many paths going out from each path, that the whole thing is untraceable. (cf. "past finding out," Rom. 11:33.)

And all of these riches, the riches of His grace, the riches of His glory, the riches of His power, are ours for the one purpose of making and keeping us holy, "that we should be to the praise of his glory."

Years ago, in the days of American slavery, there came to the lead mines of the Iowa side of the Mississippi River a slave who had been permitted by his master to make an effort to free himself, his wife and his children. In a little while he found a partner to work a mine with him. They sank a shaft to an average depth of 80 feet, but found no paying deposit of ore. This brought them to the end of his resources and exhausted the partner's endurance. The slave was able to work in the shaft only occasionally, while doing odd jobs for other miners. For a while he went on cheerfully, but hope at last began to grow dim. He therefore made up his mind to make one last effort to drill the hole as deep into the rock as possible. As he was doing so, the drill suddenly fell through, and it was not long before he had made a passage through which he let himself down into the cavern. To his unspeakable delight, upon striking a match, he was fairly dazzled by the brilliance of the crystalline ore around him, for there came the glad thought that he stood in the presence of the price that

46

would buy his freedom. But, while he had seen the value of his own freedom, he was confronted by the fact that his wife and children were still in bondage. What should he do? There were two alternatives. He could drill along the floor on the level of his discovery, or he could go deeper down for a second store of mineral wealth. The older miners advised him to follow the former course, but his heart seemed to say: "Go down! Go down! Go down!" So, down he began to drill. His intuition was soon rewarded, for he struck an opening much larger and richer than the first. This time his hopes were abundantly surpassed, and it was not long before he, with his wife and children, was emancipated, a good house erected and furnished and a large farm purchased and stocked, besides ample capital being left over for business transactions.

Now I believe that this incident is a parable of deep spiritual import. All believers know what it is to receive the forgiveness of sins, but alas, too many are content to follow the drift of a negative salvation, instead of going into the deeper experience of *a positive* salvation by possessing all the riches of their inheritance in him, for their own Christian life and for a blessing to others.

*We believe there are many sincere Christians who are living defeated lives because they are not aware of the full provision which is theirs in Christ.* Paul is always praying and writing with a burning heart, that the saints might *know* all that was involved in their *initial* acceptance of Christ as Lord and Saviour. While preaching a short time ago in a district of Texas which was filled with oil derricks, I came across a startling illustration of this truth. In the midst of a forest of oil derricks we were surprised to discover an old dilapidated frame church building which belonged to a negro congregation. For years the members of this church had struggled on in their poverty, unable even to repair and paint their building. Then suddenly, to their great surprise, oil was discovered on their property, which changed the financial status of this little group overnight! What joy, relief and new zeal came to them at the realization of their new-found wealth! What made the difference? The oil was in the ground when the property was purchased for the building. Potentially the wealth was always there; it only waited to be discovered and appropriated.

*Potentially,* every believer is filled with the Holy Ghost at the threshold of his new life in Christ, but only a few seem to know and appropriate this blessing at the time. The Holy Spirit is the executive member of the Godhead to apply the redemptive blessings of Christ to the individual believer. It is only as the believer allows the Holy Spirit to take full possession of his life that he will be able to utilize and enjoy all the provisions which are his for his Christian life. Alas, as the result of not being filled with the Spirit, there are many poverty-stricken saints being deprived of untold riches in Christ which the indwelling Spirit would minister to them, were He but permitted to fill them. The illimitable resources and immeasurable power which are potentially theirs in Christ lie idle and unused, waiting to be realized in the life by the infilling and controlling presence of the Spirit of Christ.

God's power toward us is declared in the letter to the Ephesians to be none other than that transcending might of God by which Christ was raised from the dead, exalted and enthroned at the Father's right hand. As the deliverance out of Egypt was a token of God's power on behalf of His covenant people, so Christ's resurrection exemplifies the exceeding greatness of the divine potency which is available in the Holy Spirit for the life and work of the Christian: ". . . the exceeding greatness of his power to us-ward who believe, according to the working of his  mighty power, which he wrought in Christ, when He raised him from the dead, and set him at his own right hand in the heavenly places" (Eph. 1:19-20). Think of all the possibilities and potentialities of the Spirit-filled life! How sad that many of God's dear people are willing to sell their birthright privilege for a mess of pottage!

Oh that God would send revival by the mighty power of His Spirit and deliver us from second-rate Christianity!

> *Come, Holy Spirit, heavenly Dove,*
> *With Thy all-quickening powers;*
> *Kindle a flame of sacred love*
> *In these cold hearts of ours.*
>
> *Look how we grovel here below,*
> *Fond of these trifling toys;*
> *Our souls can neither fly nor go*
> *To reach eternal joys.*
>
> *In vain we tune our formal songs,*
> *In vain we strive to rise;*
> *Hosannas languish on our tongues,*
> *And our devotion dies.*
>
> *Dear Lord, and shall we ever live*
> *At this poor dying rate?*
> *Our love so faint, so cold to Thee,*
> *And Thine to us so great?*
>
> *Come, Holy Spirit, heavenly Dove,*
> *With Thy all-quickening powers;*
> *Come, shed abroad a Saviour's love,*
> *And that shall kindle ours.*
>
> —Isaac Watts

# IV
## Constant Reviving

"The apostles had now used up their spending money,
and needed to go back to the bank of heaven for more."
—John Bunyan, commenting on Acts 4:31.

The premise of this book is that the normal condition of the Church is not revival but rather the state resulting from revival. However, we must recognize the fact that the Christian life is one of constant renewings of the Holy Spirit. As Dr. D. M. McIntyre reasons, "If we could imagine an unbroken progress of the Church, in faith and obedience, we might still suppose that she would be called to pass, at recurrent intervals, through a climacteric experience. There is always the emergence of new truths, the acceptance of fresh obligations and the realization of a richer and more elevated experience which inevitably impart an added splendor to the glory of the Bride of Christ."

It might appear on the surface that there is nothing to induce spiritual decay in the Church, but as we are too sorrowfully aware, the spiritual energy of the Church of God has ebbed and flowed like tides since the beginning. There is always a tendency to degeneration which belongs to every Christian life. Individual Christians are apt to decline from their first fervor of devotion and sacrifice to Christ, at which time the fire burns low on the altar of their heart. God has declared, "This is the law of the burnt offering. . . . The fire shall ever be burning upon the altar; it shall never go out" (Lev. 6:9, 13). Even Paul had to exhort young Timothy to "stir up the gift of God, which is in thee. . ." (2 Tim. 1:6) or to keep the fire burning brightly. Ruth Bryan, in one of her beautiful letters to a friend, says, "If the precious grace of faith be not kept in healthy exercise upon the Person and work, the sufferings and death, the blood and righteousness, of our dear Redeemer, the soul will be sure to become languid and droopy in its spiritual condition." Prayer, praise, love, joy, peace, and all other graces, will be at low water mark; and whatever external appearances or profession there may be, the heart will be conscious of distance and shyness with its Lord. You know I am writing of one who has been quickened by the Spirit and is a living soul, for we may be alive, but not lively; we may be active in our Lord's cause, but not spiritual in our own soul; we may be earnest for the salvation of others, but not be living in the joys of salvation ourselves; we may be distributing the bread and water of life but not be enjoying daily refreshment therefrom in our own experience.

The reason why I thus judge is that I find persons so lively in considering what they are doing for the Lord, yet so slow to speak of what He is doing for them. They seem delighted to tell of the great things which are happening all around but immediately shrink back if any heart subject is brought home to them. In fact, if one speaks of personal enjoyment, of the love, blood, and salvation of the Lord Jesus, there is no response from some. They put it down to the score of egotism, while others refer to years gone by when they did feel Him precious, but they confess that they know little of it now. They are so occupied in what they call "working for Him" that they hear little from Him, say little to Him, enjoy little of Him, and they can truly say, "While I was busy here and there, He was gone." It is most lamentable for any living soul to be in constant religious engagements for the good of others while "following Jesus afar off."

We see in the Acts of the Apostles that even the members of the early Church needed fresh renewings. In chapter two we find that the believers were filled with the Holy Ghost in the Upper Room. Yet in chapter four we read of their being filled once again: "And when they had prayed, the place was shaken where they were assembled together; and they were all filled with the Holy Ghost, and they spake the word of God with boldness." This does not mean that they had been living in sin and had followed the Lord afar off, but that they needed a fresh infilling for a fresh emergency that arose in their aggressive evangelism for their Blessed Redeemer. Those that were endowed *habitually* with the power of the Spirit had yet occasion for fresh supplies of the Spirit, according to the various experiences in their ministry. As John Bunyan says, "The apostles had now used up their spending money and needed to go back to the bank of heaven for more." Had these disciples not waited on the Lord for a fresh anointing, they would have been living on a fast diminishing capital which would have ended in spiritual bankruptcy.

The church at Ephesus, which had but lately thrilled with life at the touch of the Redeemer, soon languished under the pallid hand of death; and He whose eyes are as a flame of fire, whose voice is as the sound of many waters, and whose feet glow like brass molten in a furnace, comes with swift words of rebuke saying, "Remember therefore from whence thou art fallen, and *repent, and do the first works;* or else I will come unto thee quickly, and will remove thy candlestick out of his place, except thou repent" (Rev. 2:5). Here from the ascended Lord Himself is a clarion call to revival.

We would emphasize again that it is not the special spurts of the Church that count, but her steady vital ministry in her everyday life. *It is not therefore the gracious seasons of reviving that make the Church glorious and attractive, and excites the wonder of the world, but rather the abiding miracle of the steady holy walk of her members.* During the mighty days of revival in Latvia when God brought His Church out of bondage into a glorious elevated position with Christ in the Heavenlies, I discovered over a period of four years that it was necessary for us all to be periodically broken down before the Lord and to renew our vows of devotion and loyalty. There was always a tendency to relax in our fervor and to rely upon a past experience. We soon realized the necessity to watch and pray and keep abiding in Christ by the systematic reading of His Word and prompt obedience. One of the local churches that had experienced possibly the mightiest awakening of all and who saw the mighty movement of God in the salvation of souls, within nine months was found sleeping. The very first night of my series of meetings on my return to that church, I was appalled at the deadness and coldness I felt in their midst. I was heartbroken as I told the group of some five hundred believers that it was impossible for me to preach that night, and that unless they repented of their sin and came back to their "first love" we might as well close the meetings. The Spirit dealt faithfully and tenderly with them until Calvary's Love broke them down afresh before the face of the Lord God. In bitterness, humiliation, and shame they confessed that they had taken the Lord's presence for granted as He had been so gracious and glorious to them during the past months. *Their biggest sin was their presumption upon the continued unsought blessing of the Lord.* They had let their fire burn low in this careless attitude. The majority of these dear saints had been mighty intercessors, but now were seldom found in their prayer closets. I knew that drastic action was necessary, and so called at once a late prayer meeting along the line of Joel's prophecy, chapter two: "Blow the trumpet in Zion, sanctify a fast, call a solemn assembly: Gather the people, sanctify the congregation, assemble the elders, gather the children, and those that suck the breasts: let the bridegroom go forth of his chamber, and the bride out of her closet. Let the priests, the ministers of the LORD, weep between the porch and the altar, and let them say, Spare thy people, O LORD" (Joel 2:15-17). Some left the building in order to make arrangements at home for their late return. How blessed it was to see this church, with its devoted pastor, stay right on their knees until three o'clock in the morning when they could stand up together as a united group of believers and sing the doxology. Needless to say, the blessing of the Lord was outpoured the next evening in the salvation of many souls, and the tide of blessing rose higher and higher as the days went by. It was my privilege to watch this church maintain her glorious position in and for the Lord over a period of years.

When the prophet Habakkuk prayed fervently, "O Lord, revive thy work in the midst of the years," he was really praying, "O Lord, preserve Thy work! Keep it alive!" There is a simple story told of an old German friend of God which illustrates the life kept alive and glowing by the Holy Spirit. Professor Johann Albrecht Bengel was a teacher in the seminary in Denkendorf, Germany, in the eighteenth century. The seminary students used to wonder at the great intellectuality and great humility and Christ-likeness which blended their beauty in him. One night, one of them, eager to learn the secret of his holy life, slipped up into his apartment while the professor was out lecturing in the city, and hid himself behind the heavy curtains in the deep recess of the old-fashioned window. Quite a while he waited, until he grew weary and thought of how weary his teacher must be with his long hours of work in the classroom and the city. At length he heard the step in the hall, and waited breathlessly to learn the coveted secret. The man came in, changed his shoes for slippers and, sitting down at the study table, opened the old well-thumbed German Bible and began reading leisurely page by page. A half-hour he read, three-quarters of an hour, an hour and more. Then leaning his head down on his hands for a few minutes in silence he said in the simplest, most familiar way, "Well, Lord Jesus, we are on the same old terms. Good night."

Oh, that we might live such a life of unclouded fellowship with our God, always doing that which is well-pleasing to Him, depending upon His grace for our sustenance moment by moment—that ours would be a life fragrant with the very presence of God!

# V

# The Standard of the Gospel Message and Revival

"Justification gives us our title to heaven; sanctification our fitness for heaven."

—J.A.S.

"Boast not of Christ's work for you unless you can show unto us the Spirit's work in you."

—Bishop Ryle

It is our sincere and profound conviction that one of the main contributing factors to the low standard of spirituality in our churches today is the failure of the Church to preach and teach a full salvation to the lost and dying.

Somewhere down the years we have lost the knowledge of God's plan and purpose in and through the redemptive work of His beloved Son. Today the Holy Saviour is offered on God's terms of free grace, to all and sundry, irrespective of their attitude to God's holiness and to the regal claims of the majestic Christ. He is offered, may I say kindly, as One who will deliver from the penalty of sin, and yet allow the sinner to remain in love with his sins. He is presented as the Saviour of sinners, while His royal claims are ignored. The full implications of the Christian Gospel and the Christian life are entirely forgotten. The inevitable consequence of such teaching and preaching is that we have many "converts" struggling to live the Christian life who have never been born again. They have accepted the literal truth of the Gospel, but not in its living power. Their intellect has apprehended certain facts, while the heart has remained untouched. The free grace of the Gospel has been preached to them, but the standard of discipleship has been omitted. At the same time, we also have true converts who are poor examples of the redemptive power of the Gospel of the Lord Jesus.

William Cowper, at Olney, wrote with great feeling as he viewed God's glorious plan of redemption:

*Oh how unlike the complex works of man,*
*Heaven's easy, artless, unencumbered plan!*
*No meretricious graces to beguile,*
*No clustering ornaments to clog the pile;*
*From ostentation as from weakness free,*
*It stands like the cerulean arch we see,*
*Majestic in its own simplicity.*
*Inscribed above the portal, from afar,*
*Conspicuous, as the brightness of a star;*
*Legible only by the light they give,*
*Stand the soul-quick'ning words—*
*"Believe and live."*

What a multitude of false interpretations have gathered around the phrase, "Believe on the Lord Jesus." It is one of those general expressions which is capable of being explained away to mean almost anything, so that each person is tempted to put just such a meaning upon it as will include himself in the number of believers. How often, as we have spoken to people about their souls, they have told us that it was well with them; and yet, we discovered to our dismay and astonishment, that they were living in sin with no desire to live a life of holiness. They were devoid of heart-devotion to the Saviour. Surely Satan had deceived them.

Oh, Church of Christ, remember that the Gospel is a holy-making Gospel, and that the Lord Jesus is a holy Saviour! We do not live a holy life in order to be justified, but we are justified in order that we might live a holy life. The blotting out of our black past of sin is the beginning of a holy life. The root and soil of holiness is found at Calvary, where we receive from a holy and just God a full and free pardon, signed in the precious blood of Emmanuel. Horatius Bonar has wisely declared, "In this pardon and peace with God there is, of course, salvation, forgiveness, and deliverance from the wrath to come, but these, though precious, are not terminating points; not the end, but the beginning, not the top, but the bottom of that ladder, which rests its foot upon the new sepulchre wherein never man was laid, and its top against the gate of the Holy City. He, therefore, who is contenting himself with *these* has not yet learned the true purport of the Gospel; not the end which God from eternity had in view, for the sons of men, through His only begotten son; 'Who gave Himself for us that he might redeem us from all iniquity.'"

The following scriptures clearly state the purpose of the atoning death of our blessed Lord. The reader will clearly see that our Kinsman-Redeemer bore the wrath of God for us, not only that we might be acquitted, but that we also might become holy, and live a life to the praise and glory of God's grace, under the power of the lordship of Christ.

"For to this end Christ both died and rose, and revived, that he might be Lord . . ." (Rom. 14:9).

"And that he died for all, that they which live should not henceforth live unto themselves, but unto him which died for them, and rose again" (2 Cor. 5:15).

"For whom he did foreknow, he also did predestinate to be conformed to the image of his Son . . ." (Rom. 8:29).

"According as he hath chosen us in him before the foundation of the world, that we should be holy and without blame before him in love" (Eph. 1:4).

"Who gave himself for our sins, that he might deliver us from this present evil world" (Gal. 1:4).

"Who gave himself for us, that he might redeem us from all iniquity, and purify unto himself a peculiar people, zealous of good works" (Titus 2:14).

Every earnest soul-winner should prayerfully ponder our Lord's high-priestly prayer in the seventeenth chapter of

John's Gospel. Here we have the culmination of all our evangelistic effort portrayed. In those twenty-six priceless verses we have outlined for us the Father's plan and purpose for our redemption. What a high and lofty one it is!

"And all mine are thine, and thine are mine; and I am glorified in them. And now I am no more in the world, but these are in the world, and I come to thee. Holy Father, keep through thine own name those whom thou hast given me, that they may be one, as we are. . . . I have given them thy word; and the world hath hated them, because they are not of the world, even as I am not of the world. I pray not that thou shouldest take them out of the world, but that thou shouldest keep them from the evil. They are not of the world, even as I am not of the world. Sanctify them through thy truth: thy word is truth. As thou hast sent me into the world, even so have I also sent them into the world. And for their sakes I sanctify myself, that they also might be sanctified through the truth." (vv. 10-19).

Surely this mighty prayer is interpreted by Paul in Ephesians 5:25-27: ". . . Christ also loved the church, and gave himself for it; that he might sanctify and cleanse it . . . that He might present it to himself a glorious church, not having spot, or wrinkle, or any such thing; but that it should be holy and without blemish." Christ died not only to save us from future punishment but also that He might make us holy now.

"But God be thanked, that ye were the servants of sin, but ye have obeyed from the heart that form of doctrine which was delivered you. Being then made free from sin, ye became the servants of righteousness. . . . For when ye were the servants of sin, ye were free from righteousness. What fruit had ye then in those things whereof ye are now ashamed? for the end of those things is death. But now being made free from sin, and become servants to God, ye have your fruit unto holiness, and the end everlasting life" (Rom. 6:17-22).

The declaration in verse 17 is historically and experimentally true in the life of every redeemed soul. He has obeyed from the heart that form of doctrine which was delivered to him by Christ's ambassador. The word *tupos,* translated "form" in verse 17, is one of those picturesque Greek words which convey to us the deep experience of our personal salvation. The metaphor is that of the printing of a book. To produce a printed page the type is set up; the whole page is then turned into a matrix; molten lead is poured into the mould, and a solid page turned out. Then thousands of copies can be printed from the solid block, exactly like the original. The Lord Jesus Christ is God's perfect pattern. The Gospel is that mould into which the believer's life is poured, thus conforming him into the image of Christ (Rom. 8:29). Thus we see the importance of presenting to the unbeliever a full and complete Gospel.

In the third chapter of his Epistle to the Philippians the Apostle Paul sets forth the holy aspirations of every born-again person:

"But what things were gain to me, those I counted loss for Christ. Yea doubtless, and I count all things but loss for the excellency of the knowledge of Christ Jesus my Lord: for whom I have suffered the loss of all things, and do count them but dung, that I may win Christ, And be found in him, not having mine own righteousness, which is of the law, but that which is through the faith of Christ, the righteousness which is of God by faith: That I may know him, and the power of his resurrection, and the fellowship of his sufferings" (vv. 7-10).

It is an impossibility for a sinner to be justified and not sanctified. Sanctification is the inseparable consequence of regeneration. As we see in 1 Corinthians 1:30, the Lord Jesus is not only the believer's Justifier but also the Sanctifier:

"But of him are ye in Christ Jesus, who of God is made unto us wisdom, and righteousness, and sanctification, and redemption" (1 Cor. 1:30).

The unregenerate man needs not only pardon from the guilt of his sin, but cleansing from the defilement of it. The guilty sinner is redeemed that he might become holy. Bishop Ryle has warned us, "Boast not of Christ's work for you unless you can show unto us the Spirit's work in you."

C. H. Spurgeon has stated clearly, with his usual scriptural sanity: "Dear Friend, salvation would be a sadly incomplete affair, if it did not deal with the whole part of our ruined estate. We want to be purified as well as pardoned. Justification without sanctification would not be salvation at all. It would call the leper clean, and leave him to die of his disease; it would forgive the rebellion, and allow the rebel to remain an enemy of his King. It would remove the consequence but overlook the cause, and this would leave an endless and hopeless task before us. It would stop the stream for a time, but leave an open fountain of defilement which would sooner or later break forth with increased power."

What strange kind of salvation does the seeking sinner desire who cares not for holiness?

What strange kind of salvation does the seeking sinner desire who has no inclination to separate himself from sin and the world?

What strange kind of salvation does the seeking sinner desire who rebels against the lordship of Christ?

What strange kind of salvation does the seeking sinner desire who does not intend to become a bond-slave of Jesus Christ?

When a convicted sinner truly repents of his sin and receives Christ as his Lord and Saviour, a revolutionary change takes place in his heart and life. He is raised from the dead. He passes from death unto life by the quickening power of the Holy Ghost, through the supernatural Word. He is delivered from the authority of darkness and is transplanted into the Kingdom of God's dear Son. He is made fit to become partaker of the inheritance of the saints in light. He is now a child of God, having been supernaturally born again by the Spirit, into God's Family. Having been incorporated into Christ, he is a new creation. As a new creature in Christ he experiences the holy aspirations after God, for he has a propensity for holiness. All things have become new, he has a new set of appetites, and now he walks in newness of life. Because he has a new-found Saviour, he has a new name, a new Family, a new Father, a new Book, a new Song, a new Guide, and a new King. As he is now walking in the new, narrow way, he is walking in newness of life in a new direction. According to Ephesians, the second chapter, the whole course of his life has been directed into a new channel: "And you hath he quickened, who were dead in trespasses and sins; wherein *in time past ye walked according to the course of this world, according to the prince of the power of the air, the* spirit that now worketh in the children of disobedience" (vv. 1, 2). The believer is no more a stranger and a foreigner, but a fellowcitizen with the saints in the household of God, through the Spirit. Truly, old things have passed away, and all things have become new!

If a professed convert is devoid of at least some degree of holiness, some family resemblance, some devotion to Christ, he will be found wanting in God's great day of judgment. We do not deny that a new-born soul is just a babe in Christ, and that there is a growth into spiritual maturity; we do not deny that there is a deeper work of sanctification after regeneration, but we boldly affirm and strongly assert that a "convert" is not judged saved just because he himself says so. Mere lip profession is not enough; there must be clear spiritual evidence, by the sanctifying influence of the Spirit. Jonathan Edwards rightly remarks, "Holy practice is the proper evidence of saving faith." The only way a soul-winner can know that a person is saved is that he manifests the holy marks of a man whose body is the temple of the Holy Ghost and in whose heart Christ dwells. Did not our Lord warn us, in the strongest possible language, against empty professors, who profess with their mouths, but deny with their lives? "By their FRUITS ye shall know them" is His final test.

Murray McCheyne, during the mighty ingatherings of souls in Dundee and other parts of Scotland, was very careful in dealing with the hundreds of anxious souls. He was afraid of giving them false hopes and of thus damning their souls rather than saving them. As a faithful preacher of the Gospel he warned them, "Dear Friends, you may have awakenings, enlightenings, experiences, a full heart in prayers, and many signs, but if ye lack holiness you will never see the Lord. A real desire after complete holiness is the truest mark of having been born again. The Saviour first covers the soul with His white raiment, then makes the soul glorious within—restores the lost image of God, and fills the soul with pure heavenly holiness. Unregenerate men among you cannot bear this."

No matter how weak the faith, or how small are the evidences in a new-born soul, there must be some signs of divine life. If a new-born soul is united to Christ, the Head of the Church, and is "bone of his bone, and flesh of his flesh," surely he will manifest this oneness with His Lord.

One of the most profitable studies for the Christian worker is that of the word "redemption." In the Old Testament there are two words in frequent use to express the meaning of the word. The one signifies "to buy back, to redeem by payment of a ransom," and the other "to loose." In the New Testament there is only one word, but it comprises the meaning of both Hebrew words: "to release on receipt of payment." There are thus two thoughts in the word "Redemption:" the payment of a ransom, and the subsequent deliverance, i.e. our being freed. The Old Testament picture presents, then, the first part of redemption as payment by purchase. This was accomplished by the blood of the lamb (Exod. 12); but, even so, Israel was not yet redeemed, though perfectly safe under the shelter of the blood, as long as they were in Egypt. The second part, or completion of Israel's redemption, was effected when God, with a high hand and an outstretched arm, brought His people out of the land of Egypt, through the Red Sea, and then destroyed Pharaoh and all his hosts. Having been redeemed by blood and redeemed by power, they can now sing heartily of FULL SALVATION: "The Lord is my strength and song, and he is become my salvation. . . . thou hast guided them in thy strength unto thy holy habitation" (see Exod. 15:2,13). The children of Israel are now henceforth a redeemed people, never more to return to the land of bondage.

So it is today, in Gospel redemption, believers cannot be said to be redeemed until they know not only that they are sheltered by the blood but also that they are brought clean out of the enemy's land, through death and judgment, by the death and resurrection of Jesus Christ. In the example of Israel, since it was historical, the sprinkling of the blood and the crossing of the Red Sea were of necessity two successive stages. This need not be so with the believer. The death and resurrection of the Lord Jesus Christ answers both to the sprinkling of the blood and to the crossing of the Red Sea—redemption by blood, and redemption by power. Our redemption is two-fold:

the deliverance from the wrath of God, and deliverance out of the bondage of this present evil world. This should be the immediate experience of every newborn soul. And it would be far more frequently a reality in the experience of babes in Christ were a full Gospel more commonly preached.

*In full and glad surrender*
*I give myself to Thee;*
*Thine utterly and only,*
*And evermore to be.*

*0, Son of God, who lov'st me,*
*I will be Thine alone,*
*And all I have, and all I am*
*Shall henceforth be Thine own.*

*0, come and reign, Lord Jesus;*
*Rule over everything;*
*And keep me always loyal,*
*And true to Thee, my King.*

—Frances R. Havergal

# VI

## The Local Church, The Center of Revival

"Revival is an assembly word. Any movement that fails to deliver the local church from its subnormal existence and raise it to a higher elevated position in its ascended Lord has no true marks of a New Testament revival."

"God's way of revival is through renewals from within, so that our local churches become the center of blessing."

—J.A.S.

In the New Testament we discover that God's way of revival is through renewals from within, so that our local churches become the center of blessing. A true spiritual awakening will revolutionize the spiritual life of the local evangelical churches, and then in many cases will revolutionize even liberal congregations. Any movement that fails to deliver the local church from its subnormal existence and to raise it to a higher elevated position in its ascended Lord has no true marks of a New Testament revival.

How many sincere believers are ignorant of this fundamental truth! They look for revival in the great auditorium or tent, where thousands are gathered together in a glorious evangelistic effort. The heavens are open and there is a wonderful sense of the Lord's presence in their midst, which has not been known for years. "Surely," they cry, "this is revival!" However, one of the acid tests of a true spiritual awakening is that this mighty spiritual atmosphere be taken back to the local churches. For a mighty movement of the Spirit it is not enough that a few isolated individual believers be revived; the evangelical local churches must be revived. Revival, as presented to us in the New Testament, is not so much an individual experience as a collective experience of a church of born-again believers. How many times down the years we have been sadly disappointed when large united meetings, which had proved such a blessing to us all, seemed to leave the local churches untouched. The casual reader of the epistles will see that the center of all God's thought and testimony is located in these local churches. If I heard that a mighty awakening had taken place in a certain city I would not seek for revival in some great hall, rented for the purpose of evangelistic meetings; I would go directly to the evangelical churches to see the fire of God burning there.

*In the New Testament we have* God's *plan and purpose for His people in this dispensation of grace, even as we have in the Old Testament His plan and purpose for Israel.* Pentecost marked the beginning or formation of a new body or organism which is designated by Paul as "the church, which is His body" (Eph. 1:22-23). Having been incorporated into Christ by the new birth (2 Cor. 5:17), we are then incorporated into His mystical, supernatural body by the Spirit's baptism (1 Cor. 12:13). The finest description of the character and testimony of the church is to be found in Peter's first Epistle: "But ye are a chosen generation, a royal priesthood, an holy nation, a peculiar people; that ye should shew forth the praises of him who hath called you out of darkness into his marvellous light" (1 Pet. 2:9). This church is composed of all believers in the Lord Jesus, both Jew and Gentile, blessed with all spiritual blessings, sealed by the Holy Spirit individually, and baptized by the Spirit collectively. The purpose of a body is to express the character of the person who inhabits the body. The peculiar mission of the church is to express the character and life of the Son of God, and that is why a believer taught by the Spirit will always pray, "O Lord, send revival in the body of Christ!" We affirm once again that there can be no revival anywhere other than in the Body. The purpose of the Church is to gather, through her testimony of truth and love, a people who, saved by grace, and separated by the Holy Ghost from the world, are serving the Lord and waiting for His coming (1 Thess. 1).

*The Church, which is His Body, is expressed in the local churches, the members of which have been supernaturally born again and redeemed from the penalty, power, and love of sin.* In the New Testament we see the distinction between the Church universal and the "churches of the saints" (1 Cor. 14:33). These churches of the saints manifest the unity of the one glorious Church. The local church at Corinth, for example, was one part of the whole, and thus was a local expression and representation of the whole. Its members were in living spiritual union with every other member the whole world over. What a glorious and solemn truth! The evangelical believers in the Book of Acts were not detached isolated units, but were all vitally linked in fellowship with the "churches of the saints" in their district. "For by one Spirit are we all baptized into one body, whether we be Jews or Gentiles, whether we be bond or free; and have been all made to drink into one Spirit." (1 Cor. 12:13).

*In the early pages of the Book of Acts we catch the heavenly thrill of this New Testament fellowship,*

> *Christ! I am Christ's! And let the name suffice you,*
> *Ay, for me too, He greatly hath sufficed;*
> *Christ is the end, for Christ was the beginning,*
> *Christ the beginning, for the end is Christ."*
> —Meyer

There was a holy glow in the services because the living Christ was in their midst. The Son of God was absolutely everything to them. These believers were burning with love to each other because they were burning with love to their adorable Lord. "Then they that gladly received his word were baptized: and the same day there were added unto them about three thousand souls. And they continued stedfastly in the apostles' doctrine and fellowship, and in breaking of bread, and in prayers. And fear came upon every soul: and many wonders and signs were done by the apostles. And all that believed were together, and had all things common; And sold their possessions and goods, and parted them to all men, as every man had need. And they, continuing daily with one accord in the temple, and breaking bread from house to house, did eat their meat with gladness and singleness of heart, Praising God, and having favour with all the people. And the Lord added to the church daily such as should be saved" (Acts 2:41-47). "And with great power gave the apostles witness of the resurrection of the Lord Jesus: and great grace was upon them all" (4:33). "And great fear came upon all the church, and upon as many as heard these things. . . . And of the rest durst no man join himself to them: but the people magnified them. And believers were the more added to the Lord, multitudes both of men and women" (Acts 5:11,13-14). *Here is a thumbnail sketch of the type of local church that revival produces.*

IT WAS A STEADFAST CHURCH. These new-born babes continued. They continued steadfastly. Continuance is always the test of reality, and where a so-called revival cannot stand that test it is wise to inquire as to the cause of the failure. Sometimes a great desire to secure converts for publicity reasons robs the Gospel message of its drastic note. If we preach all the implications of the Evangel we may have fewer conversions but we will have genuine new-births. As Mr. Spurgeon said to his students, "If God enables you to build three thousand bricks into His spiritual temple in one day, you may do it, but Peter has been the only bricklayer who has accomplished that feat up to the present. Do not go and paint the wooden wall as if it were solid stone, but let all your building be real, substantial and true, for only this kind of work is worth doing. Let all your building for God be like that of the Apostle Paul" (1 Cor. 3:9-15).

The true mark of a real work of God is the steadfast walk, day by day, of the new-born babes. *We cannot allow that backsliding is in any sense a corollary to revival.* It is only when the emotions are greatly stirred, without a deep work of grace having been wrought in the hearts of men, that backsliding is inevitable. It is an utter impossibility to avoid deep emotion in revival, as the Holy Spirit then works mightily, bringing eternal realities so vividly before the people. But the true servants of the Lord must have their animal natures crucified, so that the emotions are under the control of the Spirit of God. The work of the Spirit is quiet and deep. Any true saint who spends hours before the Throne will know that in his closet intercession it is when he is quietest in prayer that the Spirit of God is speaking most mightily to and through him. So it is in the large gatherings. Excitement must not be aimed at. There must be something more solid. Although there was great excitement and noise in these early days of the Church's history, the excitement was as incidental as is the dust when a woman sweeps the house clean. It is the steady walk that counts.

THEY CONTINUED STEADFASTLY IN THE APOSTLES' DOCTRINE AND THE APOSTLES' FELLOWSHIP. The apostles' doctrine was the doctrine they taught and preached concerning the person and work of the Lord Jesus, the Son of God. It is also called "The doctrine of Christ" in 2 John 1:9. The apostles' fellowship consisted of all those who believed the apostles' doctrine. It is not possible to be a true member of a New Testament church without believing in the apostles' doctrine. On the other hand, if one member of the assembly denies the historic fundamentals of the Christian faith that assembly ceases to be a New Testament church. *All true revival ministry is founded on the historic truths concerning our Blessed Lord:* His eternal Sonship, His virgin birth, His sinless life, His vicarious death, His bodily resurrection, and His glorious appearing. All preaching in revival times is a reaffirmation of the fundamental truths of our glorious redemption.

Vinet, in his *Outlines of Theology,* declares: "If you learn in a general way that there has been a revival in a place, that Christianity is reanimated, that faith has become living, and that zeal abounds—do not ask in what soil, in what system, these precious plants grow. You may be sure beforehand that it is in the rough and rugged soil of orthodoxy, under the shade of those mysteries which confound human reasoning. . . . The revival has preached the total depravity of man and his powerlessness to save himself. The revival has preached salvation by grace and not by works, the necessity of the new birth in order to enter into the Kingdom of Heaven, and the absolute dependence of man in regard to God. The revival has preached the plenary and essential deity of Jesus Christ as well as His perfect and entire humanity; it has declared that God was in Jesus Christ, reconciling the world unto Himself; and that it is in Jesus Christ alone that we have remission of sins and access to the Father; and that whosoever abideth not in Him abideth in death."

In Ephesians 2:20 we are told that the Church was "built upon the foundation of the apostles and prophets, Jesus Christ himself being the chief cornerstone." This means that the Church was founded upon the teaching of the apostles and prophets concerning the Lord Jesus Christ. Therefore the Church was founded upon doctrine. So in a New Testament church the Word of God will be honored and obeyed. Such will be not only a Bible-believing but a Bible-loving church. Its leaders will expound the truths of the Word of God from Genesis to Revelation. Its members will have a deep appreciation and spiritual penetration into divine Truth. Their Christian life will not be based merely upon their own experiences. They will be deep students of the Word. They will not remain babes, but will rather become giants as they digest the strong meat of the Word. How sad it is today to see around us so many believers who hardly spend a half-hour a day studying the Word for themselves. How few believers can even give a clear explanation of the truth of "adoption," and yet this is one of the most vital truths in the Christian life. Too many of our church members remain immature babes, requiring to be spoon-fed by their pastors for many years.

IT WAS A PRAYERFUL CHURCH. When I was a young convert the first thing that struck me when reading the Acts of the Apostles was the fact that these local assemblies lived in the atmosphere of prayer. Prayer meetings were the order of the day. They prayed on every occasion. They prayed for open doors. They prayed for guidance and boldness in their ministry after they had passed through the open doors. They prayed before the battle, during the battle, and after the battle. They prayed that God would show them His plan and that He would frustrate Satan's plan. They prayed that God would raise up workers. They prayed that God would empower workers. They prayed that God would send forth workers. They prayed in prison, and they prayed themselves out of prison. They prayed in their homes and they prayed in their church gatherings. They prayed in their private circles, and they prayed before the Sanhedrin. They lived on their knees.

In order that the apostles might "give themselves continually to prayer" they appointed seven men of honest report to administer the secular business of the church. So mighty were they in prayer that they "turned the world upside down."

*A true New Testament church will always be mighty in prayer.* Said George Mueller, when writing to Hudson Taylor in China, "If you are going to take that province for Christ, you must go forward on your knees." One of our desperate needs is the revival of the weeknight prayer meeting. How often I have heard the remark, "Only a prayer meeting." What is inferred by such a statement? Surely it implies that there is nothing important or interesting doing, as the Christians are only going to talk with God! One of the mightiest manifestations of the Spirit in revival power is the resurrection of dead prayer meetings. The majority of pastors would be pleasantly shocked and surprised if even 50 per cent of their congregation turned out for the weeknight prayer meeting.

IT WAS AN OVERFLOWING CHURCH. They overflowed in liberality and praise. They overflowed in *liberality* because they overflowed in love. Their cups ran over with love to the Lord Jesus. They knew the significance of the high cost of their redemption. Gazing at Calvary, they could not hoard up their money and hold on to their lands and houses. The original text reveals that they *continued* to sell their property and goods and *continued* to bring the money and place it at the feet of the apostles. It was not mere passing excitement, or the flush of a first love; it was a deep, deep realization of the glory of their salvation that caused them to give so generously. If they had lived in our day, they would have sung heartily:

> *Everybody should know—everybody should know,*
> *I have such a wonderful Saviour, that everybody*
> *should know!*

What a great challenge to us today! *If these Christians in the first century needed to sell their possessions for the evangelization of a lost and dying world, how much more we who live in the twentieth century!* While vast continents still lie in midnight darkness, and hundreds of millions have never heard the Gospel, surely if our hearts were filled with His love and His passion we would show forth the same response. "I warn you," said A. J. Gordon, "that it will go hard with you at the judgment seat if He finds your wealth hoarded up in needless accumulations instead of being sacredly devoted to giving the Gospel to the lost."

They overflowed in *praise.* Their whole life was flooded with praise. The assembly gatherings were characterized by praise. They praised God for His glorious salvation They praised Him that they were counted worthy to be ambassadors of the Lord Jesus. They praised Him that they could suffer shame and reproach for His glory. They praised Him that they had something to sacrifice for the spread of the Gospel. Deep spirituality and worship go hand in hand. Read the hymns of the past centuries in English, French, German, Russian, Scandinavian, and Latin. Read the hymns that were born in the high days of the Church. How they overflow with deep spiritual insight and simplicity of adoration to Christ.

> *O God, I love Thee; not that my poor love*
> *    May win me entrance to Thy heaven above,*
> *Nor yet that strangers to Thy love must know*
> *    The bitterness of everlasting woe.*
>
> *But Jesus, Thou art mine, and I am Thine;*
> *    Clasped to Thy bosom by Thy arms divine,*
> *Who on the cruel cross for me hast borne*
> *    The nails, the spear, and man's unpitying scorn.*

*No thought can fathom, and no tongue express*
  *Thy grief, Thy toils, Thy anguish measureless;*
*Thy death, O Lamb of God, the undefiled—*
  *And all for me, Thy wayward sinful child!*

*How can I choose but love Thee, God's dear Son,*
  *O Jesus, loveliest and most loving one!*
*Were there no heaven to gain, no hell to flee,*
  *For what Thou art alone, I must love Thee.*

*Not for the hope of glory or reward,*
  *But even as Thyself hast loved me, Lord*
*I love Thee, and will love Thee and adore*
  *Who art my King, my God, for evermore.*

How little praise there is in our churches today! How refreshing it would be for a group of churches to come together for a united praise meeting. Such words related to the word "praise" as price, prize, precious, appraise, appreciate, etc., help us to understand better the full meaning of the term. The saints bursting forth spontaneously into songs of adoration and worship is one of the glories of revival. Song leaders are not necessary during such times, as the huge congregations sing over and over again the songs of Zion which spring from their hearts. I remember once dismissing an immense congregation in Czechoslovakia twice in a single evening without any success. I had finished preaching and pronounced the benediction twice, but the believers went on praising the Lord for over an hour after I had left the building. In times of revival the Holy Spirit inspires a great number of hymns to be written. For every John Wesley there is a Charles Wesley:

*Oh, for a thousand tongues to sing*
  *My great Redeemer's praise!*

*The glories of my God and King,*
*The triumphs of His grace.*

IT WAS A POWERFUL CHURCH. *It was powerful in its Gospel presentation.* In one day three thousand souls were saved, and on another day about five thousand men and women. Today if a church of three thousand members won one hundred and twenty souls to Christ in one day some would call that revival! Oh, dear child of God, a church that is not a Soul-winning church is not a New Testament church. It is true that there are times of sowing as well as times of reaping, but every pastor and every group of believers should search their hearts industriously to see why there is a dearth of conversions. It seems that Satan has so drugged the Lord's dear ones that they have no deep concern and anguish in their lack of spiritual results. How many assemblies accept with astonishing calmness annual reports of so few, if any, conversions! Such churches should convene special meetings in desperation before the Lord to see if there is anything hindering God's blessing His Word according to Acts 4:33, "And with great power gave the apostles witness of the resurrection of the Lord Jesus: and great grace was upon them all."

How inconsistent it is for churches back home, who very rarely ever see the Lord add to their membership, to expect a mighty harvest to be reaped by the missionaries they support laboring in hostile heathen lands! If they demand and expect a mighty manifestation of the power of the Gospel among the pagan population, should they not expect a mightier demonstration in an evangelical atmosphere?

*They were powerful in their holiness.* "And great fear came upon all the church, and upon as many as heard these things. And by the hands of the apostles were many signs and wonders wrought among the people; (and they were all with one accord in Solomon's porch. And of the rest durst no man join himself to them: but the people magnified them. And believers were the more added to the Lord, multitudes both of men and women.)" (Acts 5:11-14). It was a powerful church because of the presence of the Holy Spirit in their midst. The sin of Ananias and Sapphira was a frontal attack by Satan to deny the deity of the Holy Spirit. When judgment was brought to bear upon these two, a holy awe fell upon saved and unsaved alike. So holy was this church that hypocrites and unbelievers dared not join themselves to it. On the other hand, crowds of men and women who were true believers were brought in.

*How easy it is to receive the "right hand of fellowship" in our churches today! Without doubt this weakness is one of the underlying causes of the subnormal church.* Too many people are rushed to the altar. Too many people are rushed into church membership without careful examination and instruction. In our evangelical churches of Eastern Europe and Russia, sometimes it takes from six months to a year for a new convert to be received into church membership. So holy and powerful are these churches in their Gospel witness that the unsaved attending their services know that it is no small thing to enlist under the banner of the Lord and identify themselves with a company of born-again believers.

One of the mightiest warnings of A. J. Gordon to the church is as follows: "We dwell much upon the attractions of Christianity, but rarely stop to think that it may also have repulsions, which are vitally necessary to its purity and permanence. If the Church of Christ draws to herself that which she cannot assimilate to herself, her life is at once imperiled; for the body of believers must be at one with itself, though it be at war with the world. Its purity and its power depend, first of all, upon its unity. So that if, perchance, the Church shall attract without at the same time transforming them; if she shall attach them to her membership without assimilating them to her life—she has only weakened herself by her increase, and diminished herself by her additions. Such is the lesson that is impressed upon us by the text 'and of the rest durst no man join himself to them.'"

"The Church has just entered upon her first conquest. The Gospel is preached with a freeness and breadth of offer unheard of before. Three thousand souls have been added to the Church in a single day. The tide of success is rising higher and higher. The sect of the Nazarenes is fairly becoming popular. Multitudes are crowding up to lay their gifts at the apostles' feet. Is there not a danger that the infant Church may be overwhelmed in the tide of her own prosperity? That upon the swelling wave of success the uncircumcised and the unclean may be born into her communion to corrupt and destroy it? But look! Like a keen lightning flash the judgment of God falls in the midst of His mercies, and the two who had *agreed together to tempt the Spirit of the Lord* lie dead at the apostles' feet. Is God about to close the gate of mercy so recently opened, and to guard it with a flaming sword? No! Here is an exhibition of His holiness in the midst of His free grace. And before this unsheathed sword of His holiness the multitude instantly divides—a part thrust back, a part drawn nearer. No sincere disciples are repelled, for the record is that '. . . believers were the more added to the Lord, multitudes both of men and women.'

"The terror of the Lord puts afar off those who have not the love of the Lord to bring them nigh. My brethren, I know of no lesson concerning the growth and development of Christ's Church that needs to be more thoughtfully pondered than this. The tendency of our times is to multiply the attractions of Christianity. No attraction can be too powerful, no charm can be too alluring that acts for the single ends of drawing believers to Christ and identifying them with His Body. *But the appeals which win men without transforming them, which join them to the Church without bringing them into fellowship with Christ, are fatal to a pure Christianity, and in the end must put the very existence of the Church in jeopardy.* In the first place, the sanctity of life and character which Christ requires in His Church is her most powerful defence. These, O Church of God, are thy weapons of defence and conquest! I believe that the most effective discipline which any church can have is a consecrated and devoted and unworldly piety in its members."

Whenever we see God's wonderful pattern for the Church so practically demonstrated in these pages in the Book of Acts we cry with Jeremiah, "How is the gold become dim! how is the most fine gold changed! . . ." (Lam. 4:1a).

# VII
## Believing for Revival

"As long as the blessed Holy Spirit, Himself the great standing miracle, abides and works on the earth, the Church's potential is the same as it was in the apostolic days.

"A subnormal and backslidden church is an insult and a disgrace to a holy, powerful God."

—J.A.S.

There are many sincere saints of God who believe that the days of revival are past. They base their assertions on the fact that the Word of God predicts that "in the last days perilous times shall come," when there will be a wholesale departure from the faith. They admit that the Gospel has lost none of its ancient power to save, and that here and there a few souls will be gathered in, but they believe that there will be no outpourings of the Holy Spirit before the rapture of the Church. This being so, they argue that it is completely out of the plans and purposes of God for the Church to pray for and expect a mighty revival. Such teaching has wrought incalculable harm to a subnormal church and encouraged the sleeping saints in their indolence when they ought to be claiming the promises of God for awakening in their midst.

It is true that one sees evidences of the denial of the faith all about him. The majority of our large denominations are preaching "another Gospel," as spoken of by Paul in Galatians 1:8. Too many Protestant pastors deny the fundamentals of our historic Christian faith. Yet, in spite of all this, we assert that the day of miracles is not past. *As long as the blessed Holy Spirit, Himself the great standing miracle, abides and works on the earth the Church's potential is the same as it was in the apostolic days. Our* divine Paraclete has never been withdrawn, and He still waits to work gloriously through clean, obedient vessels.

Dr. Robert C. McQuilkin has left us this warning:

"Let us not limit God in His working, and let us not fail to be ready for new and great outpourings of the Holy Spirit in the closing days of this age. For the days are upon us when nothing will avail to break through the overwhelming power of the enemy, except supernatural power beyond what most Christians have known anything about. If the Church was supernaturally blessed of God at its birth, who will say that, in the closing days of its witness here on earth before its translation, it will not be blessed in even a mightier way?"

*The very fact that God is sending local revivals in different parts of the world in answer to the heart-longing of His people surely renders false the doctrine that He does not purpose to send revival in these last days. If* God is reviving His work and His people in other places, then why not in your church, your city, your town, your country?

It is the Holy Spirit of God who inspires the saints of God to long for and claim revival in their midst. The very fact that one sees individuals and small groups in every place whose hearts have been burdened with the low spiritual condition of the Church and who are crying to Him for His supernatural working in their midst is proof enough that the days of His miraculous workings have not passed. Even as God is not mocked, so He does not mock His own. Jonathan Edwards has said, "When God is about to do a mighty new thing He always sets His people praying."

*Not only has the Spirit, the Lord of the Harvest, burdened many hearts to pray and long for revival in their midst, He has raised up and sent forth into His vineyard fearless prophets with a burning message and call for repentance to the Church today.* The message God has given to these holy men and women is an uncomfortable one, which tends to insult the lukewarm Church and infuriate her cold, sleeping members. It is a message which will not compromise with the sinful, selfish, fruitless, powerless condition which characterizes God's people. Like the prophet Ezekiel, these special anointed messengers are "for a sign" to a disobedient, rebellious Church. Having been broken down themselves before the Lord, and having been shown the abominations of Zion, and having literally digested the message of God until it is their very own, they have now become living, vital representatives of the message in their lives (see Ezek. 12:11). "They are men wondered at" (Zech. 3:8). They are crucified with Christ, dead to their own feelings, and fear not the face of a stiff-necked generation (Jer. 1:8). Their message rudely awakens and disturbs the saints, as the thought of "the Master of the House" coming suddenly and interrupting all their plans is far from welcome, and they rise up in protest. The message of the prophet of revival can never be a popular one, since the Holy God commands, "Cry aloud, spare not, lift up thy voice like a trumpet, and shew my people their transgression, and the house of Jacob their sins" (Isa. 58:1).

We cannot believe that the day of miracles is past. *On the contrary, it is now time for God to work in an overwhelmingly mighty way in these last days of a dying dispensation of grace.* Millions yet lie in heathen darkness, outside of Christ. Christ's Body must be made complete, and it must surely be His will that His Body be composed of peoples from every realm, and tribe and nation. Only a cold, narrow-visioned believer could think that the Body of Christ could be composed mainly of the white race. If the dying pagan millions are ever to hear the Gospel for even the first time, there must be a mighty upheaval in the Church back home. Something revolutionary must take place in the hearts and lives of God's people which will arouse them from their complacency and send them out in obedience to His command to "Go!"

*The greatest reason for my belief that God wants to send revival in these days, however, has to do with His plans and purposes for the lives of His redeemed ones.* God is never content in any age for His people to live below the standard which He has set for His Son's Bride. Such passages from His Word as "Begin at My sanctuary (Ezek. 9:6), "Blow ye the trumpet in Zion" (Joel 2:1), and "Remember therefore from whence thou art fallen, and repent, and do the first works; or else I will come unto thee quickly, and will remove thy candlestick out of his place, except thou repent" (Rev. 2:5) remind us that God is never content with the subnormal life of the Church. There is no parent who would be satisfied or happy about his children's being sick and perennially low in health. It would indeed be startling, upon asking a father concerning the health of his children, to hear him say, "Most of the time my children are weak and sickly, but it doesn't matter, because for a few weeks each year they come back to normal and are rather healthy." No man is satisfied that his bride be subnormal either physically or mentally. Far less can our Father be content for one moment to see His Church anything less than holy and powerful, living in vital communion with Himself, as He has purposed. A subnormal and backslidden Church is an insult and a disgrace to a holy, powerful, almighty God.

The Lord is angry with His people. "The Lord hath also a controversy with Judah, and will punish Jacob according to his ways; according to his doings will He recompense him" (Hos. 12:2). The Lord has a solemn indictment against His people: "For my people have committed two evils; they have forsaken me the fountain of living waters, and hewed them out cisterns, broken cisterns, that can hold no water" (Jer. 2:13).

92

*Let any group of believers who have any hesitancy as to whether God wants to bless them in a deeper, fuller way or no, go aside and fast and pray believingly, according to the divine formula as outlined for us in the prophecy of Joel:*

"Blow the trumpet in Zion, sanctify a fast, call a solemn assembly: Gather the people, sanctify the congregation, assemble the elders, gather the children, and those that suck the breasts: let the bridegroom go forth of his chamber, and the bride out of her closet. Let the priests, the ministers of the Lord, weep between the porch and the altar, and let them say, Spare Thy people, O Lord, and give not Thine heritage to reproach, that the heathen should rule over them: wherefore should they say among the people, Where is their God?" (Joel 2:15-17).

Without a shadow of doubt, if God's people will meet His conditions in this way, and for this cause, He will send them times of revival:

"Then will the Lord be jealous for his land, and pity his people. Yea, the Lord will answer and say unto his people, Behold, I will send you corn, and wine, and oil, and ye shall be satisfied therewith: and I will no more make you a reproach among the heathen. . . . Fear not, O land; be glad and rejoice: for the Lord will do great things. . . . Be glad then, ye children of Zion, and rejoice in the Lord your God: for he hath given you the former rain moderately, and he will cause to come down for you the rain, the former rain, and the latter rain in the first month. And the floors shall be full of wheat, and the fats shall overflow with wine and oil. And I will restore to you the years that the locusts have eaten, the cankerworm, and the caterpiller, and the palmerworm, my great army which I sent among you. And ye shall eat in plenty, and be satisfied, and praise the name of the Lord your God, that hath dealt wondrously with you: and my people shall never be ashamed" (Joel 2:18-26).

There are those who declare that the prophecy of Joel is for Israel as a nation, and has nothing whatsoever to do with the Church. We believe, however, with men of such mature judgment as Jonathan Edwards, A. T. Pierson, and F. B. Meyer, that this passage predicts also a mighty movement of the Holy Spirit in the last days before the Rapture. It is very noticeable that the apostle Peter did not say on the day of Pentecost, when quoting this great prophecy, that this was the fulfillment of what had been spoken by the prophet Joel. There is no mistaking the language that he used. Instead of saying, "This is the fulfillment of what Joel said," he declared, "This is that which was spoken by the prophet Joel." What Peter was really declaring to the awe-struck crowd was this: "This Pentecost is only a foretaste; the great fulfillment of Joel's words are yet to come. There is to be a greater Pentecost, of which this is only the few first-drops that precede the abundant rain."

If God was a jealous God for His earthly people, how much more is He jealous for us who have been purchased at such a price to be entirely possessed by His Son for a spiritual Bride. And if God was delighted to hear the repentant confessions and anxious cries of His people of old, how much more can we not expect Him to respond to the believing prayers of His heavenly Bride!

The pages of Holy Writ are flooded with challenging verses direct from the Throne, which ought to drive us to our knees in prayer and expectation, that they may become real in our own lives. *And when God answers such prayers of faith and fulfils His Word to those who claim them, revival has come!* Among such challenging calls are:

"Call unto Me, and I will answer thee, and shew thee great and mighty things, which thou knowest not" (Jer. 33:3).

"Sanctify yourselves: for to morrow the Lord will do wonders among you" (Jos. 3:5).

"Prove me now herewith, saith the Lord of hosts, if I will not open you the windows of heaven, and pour you out a blessing, that there shall not be room enough to receive it. And I will rebuke the devourer for your sakes, and he shall not destroy the fruits of your ground; neither shall your vine cast her fruit before the time in the field, saith the Lord of hosts" (Mal. 3:10-11).

"He that believeth on me, as the scripture hath said, out of his belly shall flow rivers of living water" (John 7:38).

Some, of course, will object that the above-mentioned portions come from the Old Testament and are not really challenges and promises for us today. As one wonderfully answers such objections: "I could go from one end of the Bible to another, and produce an astonishing variety of texts that are applicable as promises; enough to prove that in whatever circumstances a child of God may be placed, God has provided in the Bible some promise, either general or particular, which he can apply, that is precisely suited to his case. Many of God's promises are very broad on purpose to cover much ground. What can be broader than the promise 'What things soever ye desire when ye pray, etc.?' What praying Christian is there who has not been surprised at the length and breadth and the fullness of the promises of God when the Spirit has applied them to his heart? Who that lives the life of prayer has not wondered at his own blindness, at not having before seen and felt the extent of meaning and richness of these promises, when viewed under the light of the Spirit of God? At such time he has been astonished at his own ignorance, and has found the Spirit applying the promises and declarations of the Bible in a sense of which he had never before dreamed of their being applicable.

"The manner in which the apostles applied the promises and prophecies and declarations of the Old Testament places in a strong light the breadth of meaning, and fullness, and richness of the Word of God. He that walks in the light of God's countenance, and is filled with the Spirit of God as he ought to be, will often make an appropriation of promises to himself and application of them to his own circumstances, and the circumstances of those for whom he prays, that a blind professor of religion would never dream of making. A curious case occurred in one of the towns of the western part of the state of New York. There was a mighty revival there. A certain clergyman came to visit the place, and heard a great deal said about the Prayer of Faith. He was staggered at what they said, for he had never regarded the subject in the light in which they did. He inquired about it of the minister that was laboring there. The minister requested him, in a kind spirit, to go home and take his Testament, look out the passages that referred to prayer and go round to his most praying people, and ask of them how they understood these passages. He did so. Going to his praying men and women, and reading the passages, without note or comment, he asked them what they thought. He found that their plain common sense had led them to understand these passages and to believe that they meant just what they say. This affected him, and the fact of his presenting the promises before their minds awakened the spirit of prayer in them, and revival followed."

One *great obstacle that hinders the working of God is the fact that so many pastors and other Christian workers do not believe in the power of God to fulfil His precious promises.* What evangelist has not heard "the platitudinous Shibboleth," as Hyman Appelman calls it, upon being invited for a series of evangelistic services, of being told by the leaders on the very first day of arrival, "We do not want to discourage you, but we feel it is only fair that you should know the facts about our city. It is the most Gospel-hardened city in the world. The situation here is like nowhere else in the nation. The conditions that exist in our local churches are very peculiar. They do not exist elsewhere. We are afraid that there is not going to be much blessing." When I hear such words, I reply quietly, "Of course your situation is difficult and peculiar, but so are all spiritual situations. The situation is extraordinary, but we have an extraordinary God! The basic needs of any group of the Lord's people are the same in any nation and in any language." Surely someone is mistaken in his assertions, because all Christian leaders maintain that *their* city is the graveyard of evangelists! I have found in my thirty-three years of ministry that these so-called "graveyards" are wonderful places to desperately cry, "Thus saith the Lord God; Come from the four winds, O breath, and breathe upon these slain, that they may live" (Ezek. 37:9). I have found that these "graveyards" have in many instances given God a chance, if I may say it reverently, to exhibit His mighty power in the resurrection of "dry bones" (Ps. 106:8).

Such Christians are defeated *before* they begin their campaign. They do not believe that God can win the victory because of the great odds against them. No wonder their prayers are never answered, as they pray without faith. The Apostle James says, "He that wavereth is like a wave of the sea driven with the wind and tossed. For let not that man think that he shall receive anything of the Lord" (James 1:6,7). Their unbelief is a stumblingblock to new-born babes as well as to the unsaved. Early in my Christian life I was greatly impressed and helped by an incident I read in the life of Charles Finney. Although unsaved, he was a regular attendant at a church in

97

New York State. He took part in the services of the church, and even attended the prayer meetings. One prayer meeting night, when the church was ready to go on its knees, someone asked the young lawyer, "Mr. Finney, would you like us to pray for you?"

"No, I would not," was his reply.

"Why not?"

"Because it would do no good. I live in this community. I attend this church regularly, and I never see God answering your prayers. I hear you pray for revival, but God never sends revival. Your prayers are not effective."

Nazareth was the most privileged place in our Saviour's lifetime. He spent nearly thirty of the thirty-three years of His life here on earth in that town. One would think that in no place would the mighty God want to manifest His power as in Nazareth. But the people of Nazareth are known the world over for their unbelief. The evangelist Mark says, "And He could there do no mighty work, save that He laid His hands on a few sick folk, and healed them" (Mark 6:5). To lay His hands on a few sick folk and heal them was not accounted as any mighty thing. Christ longed to do greater things for them. What was wrong? A chilling fog of unbelief had swept over the whole community. "He marvelled because of their unbelief" (Mark 6:6). They saw no mighty works because the necessary conditions for their performance was lacking.

In the life of Abraham we have a striking illustration of the power of faith claiming the promises of God in an impossible situation. He had received a direct promise from the living God that he would have a son. He knew it was a human impossibility for him and Sarah to have a son at their age. Yet, under hopeless circumstances he hopefully believed. He kept on believing in spite of all the Satanic assaults on his faith. "And being not weak in faith, he considered not his own body now dead, when he was about an hundred years old, neither yet the deadness of Sara's womb: He staggered not at the promise of God through unbelief; but was strong in faith, giving glory to God; And being fully persuaded that, what he had promised, he was able also to perform" (Rom. 4:19-21).

His faith never quailed. There was no feebleness in his faith. *Under utterly hopeless circumstances he hopefully believed, being absolutely certain that whatever God had promised, He was bound by, and He was able also to make it good.* So mighty was his faith that "he gave glory to God." He gave glory to God before the promise was fulfilled. It would have been easy to give glory to God after the child was born; it is easy to give the shout of faith after prayer is answered. We remember that the children of Israel had to give the triumphant shout of faith before the walls of Jericho would fall flat before them.

> *Faith, mighty faith, the promise sees,*
> *And looks to God alone;*
> *Laughs at impossibilities,*
> *And cries, "It shall be done!"*

The Holy Spirit would never have recorded this incident in the life of Abraham if it were not fraught with great spiritual import. "For whatsoever things were written aforetime were written for our learning, that we through patience and comfort of the scriptures might have hope" (Rom. 15:4).

*We sing lustily in our gatherings, "Standing on the promises of Christ, my King," but, my dear brother and sister, we cannot stand on the promises until we have fallen on our knees and claimed them before God's face.* And once we have claimed them at the Throne of Grace for ourselves, and asked

God to make them real in our experience, we must arise and virtually walk over all the unoccupied, unclaimed, untrodden territory of God's promises until they are truly performed in us. Remember the Word of the Lord to Joshua: "Every place that the sole of your foot shall tread upon, that have I given unto you" (Joshua 1:3). Before the Land of Promise could become theirs, the Children of Israel had to walk through the length and breadth of it and measure it off foot by foot (by their own feet). It is interesting to note that they only measured off one-third of the territory God had given them, and consequently they never possessed more than that. They *possessed only that which they measured off, and no more.* How glorious are the precious promises of God to His people! They are as true in these apostate days as they were in the days in which they were spoken. How very few of us have ever conceived the wealth and extent of the land, and how very few of us have ever taken possession of the promises of God in the all-conquering Name of the Lord Jesus!

William C. Burns, who was mightily used of God in Scotland and in China, lived in the constant expectation of a coming revival to his beloved land of Scotland. As a young man of only twenty-three years, he had read the Scriptures on his knees, and pleaded on his knees, and believed on his knees, that God was going to open the windows of heaven and pour out such a blessing that there would be not enough room to receive it. His brother relates of him, "He had indeed, as I distinctly remember, very exalted views of what might be expected, even in these latter days, from the outpouring of the Spirit, in answer to the earnest prayers of a revived church. His mind had dwelt much in common with many others at that time on the divine promises to that effect, and on the grand typical fulfillment of them on the Day of Pentecost. That memorable scene he regarded not as an isolated event but as a pattern of what the Church might hope in any age to see. It might even be more glorious. Even some of the most startling outward manifestations of the Spirit's working then displayed he regarded not as exceptional circumstances but as what might be repeated any day before our eyes. The cloven tongues and the gift of many languages may have passed away, but the cries of stricken consciences and the loud sobs of broken hearts belong more or less wherever in a congregated multitude of sinful men the arrows of the mighty King are sharp in the hearts of His enemies.

"I remember having a discussion with him on this very subject in the course of a quiet walk from Glasgow toward our home in Kilsyth, shortly before he commenced his work in Dundee. I ventured to question whether, even though the working of the divine Spirit in the bosom of a Christian congregation were as powerful and profound as in Pentecostal times, the habitual reserve and self-restraint of modern life, especially among the more educated classes, would not prevent such unrestrained expression of inward feeling as that displayed at Pentecost. To this he demurred, deeming that if the mighty rushing wind, which bloweth where it listeth, should indeed come with power, we should hear the sound thereof so that even the world itself should not be wholly able to close its ears. Little did I think that within a month or two of that time, and in the parish church of that very place to which we were then bending our steps, I should myself witness what seemed so remarkable a verification of his words!"

At this time Burns was supplying for Murray McCheyne in Dundee during the latter's absence to the Holy Land. It was under his preaching on the 23rd day of July 1839 that the great revival of Kilsyth took place. He had gone from Dundee on a weekday to his father's church in Kilsyth to preach with him, when suddenly "the Holy Ghost fell." All Scotland heard the glad news that the sky was no longer brass; the windows of heaven had opened!

*In my own ministry, covering a period of thirty-four years, I have known individuals, or a group of believers, to search the Scriptures diligently to see if there were any bright hope which would enlighten their spiritual darkness of defeat and discouragement.* Again and again they have been led by the Spirit to see that all God's promises are "Yea and Amen in Christ Jesus," and that these promises are for them today, even though they may have been addressed to God's people in bygone days; that the whole body of Scripture had set down a divine set of principles which govern all God's dealings with His people. These believers did not have a mutilated Bible, where there is little left for the believers in these last days. They embraced all the promises. They stood on them, and modestly yet fearlessly proclaimed in faith that God was going to send a mighty spiritual awakening. They believed that the moral lessons taught by the Lord to His disciples in olden days had a deep spiritual significance for them in these later times. Over and over I have seen the Lord work mightily in answer to the believing prayers of these dear saints in many lands.

The story behind Mr. Moody's successful revival ministry in Britain is an illustration of the prayer of faith for revival. Having been greatly blessed through the writings of C. H. Spurgeon and the mighty exploits of faith by George Mueller, Mr. Moody came to Britain with the express purpose of meeting these two brethren. So far as we know, God's servant spoke only once during this visit. His next visit took place in 1862, during the erection of his new church building which was to replace the one which had been destroyed by the great Chicago fire. He greatly needed a rest, and had no intention of conducting meetings. After his arrival, however, he was persuaded to take the Sunday services at a Congregational Church where the Rev. T. Lessey was minister. It was a very ordinary Lord's Day morning service, with no unusual response. But at the close of the evening service there was an unexpected movement, when large numbers flocked to the inquiry room. As the people separated, Mr. Moody announced that the pastor would be in the church vestry on the following evening to meet those who desired to receive Christ as Lord and Saviour. Hundreds responded to the invitation, and they came the next night and the next. There was no advertising and no committees, as the work was spontaneous. *D. L. Moody was relatively unknown.* The work went on so mightily that Mr. Lessey had to telegraph Mr. Moody, who had gone to Dublin, to please return and help him gather in the harvest. Four hundred persons came into full fellowship with this evangelical church alone.

Naturally both evangelist and pastor were deeply perplexed as to the cause of this unusual blessing. They held long conversations together to try and unravel the mystery. Their own faith had not been high in expectation. Then they learned the secret. There were two sisters, members of the congregation, one of whom was bedridden. These two had prayed persistently for a long time that God would send Mr. Moody to preach to their congregation. One sister, on returning from the morning service, could hardly wait to report the startling news to the invalid, that D. L. Moody had preached from the pulpit that morning. It was then plain that God had now answered their prayers. They spent the whole afternoon and evening before the Lord in great fear and trembling, praising Him for His goodness.

This remarkable work of grace was the means of giving Moody an open door to the entire British nation.

Whenever revival has broken out during the course of our own ministry we have always searched quietly and reverently to discover what individual or group of believers had been embracing the promises. We know that revival does not come because of the eloquence of great preachers, or because of the power of a great organization. *It is the supernatural, spontaneous work of God, which commences* in *the secret place of intercession, because some believers dare to believe that God can fulfil His word even today.* (Revival never begins with a great noise or with great crowds.) I could give countless illustrations of this blessed fact. I have known of whole groups of churches lifted up to a high standard of holiness and thousands of souls saved as the result of a few believers who held on to God to do a "new thing" (Isa. 43:19).

One day in a northern city of Eastern Europe (now in Soviet Russia) I was concerned because, for no apparent reason, God had suddenly sent revival. In other cities and countries it usually comes after several weeks or even months of throne ministry. But here on the fifth day, the heavens were rent asunder, and we were deluged with heaven-sent blessing. One thousand believers packed the church building each morning for Bible study. Thousands heard the Gospel in the evening in a larger auditorium. So great was the hunger for the Word among the unsaved that there was no room for the believers in the evening service. I asked them to go to their own churches and pray and not take up the seats which should be occupied with unsaved. The spiritual distress among the unsaved was great, as the Sword of the Spirit stabbed their hearts night after night. It was midnight and after before I could leave the building. I was greatly disturbed in my mind and could not sleep, being at a loss to explain the "open windows" (Mal. 3:10). I had arrived unheralded and unknown, only by the invitation of the Holy Spirit. The meetings had commenced on a Friday night with some seven people at a prayer meeting!

One evening the Lord very kindly allowed me to discover the secret of the blessing. Being afraid that I would not have sufficient power of the Spirit to proclaim the Evangel to the thousands who had gathered, I made my way to the basement of the auditorium in order to have a few minutes more of prayer. I began to pray in the darkness, but it was not long before I felt an overwhelming sense of the majesty of God. I knew right away there was someone else in the large basement, praying. I quietly put on the light, and there I saw at the extreme end of the basement some twelve sisters, flat on their faces before God! They were totally unaware of my presence. They were "inside the veil," touching the Throne, by the power of the Spirit, while upstairs God was working mightily among the unsaved.

OH, FOR GOD TO RAISE UP A MIGHTY BAND WHO WILL DARE TO BELIEVE GOD FOR REVIVAL!

# VIII
## The Promise of Revival

"Search and see, look in the Book and read; was there any who did trust Him that was put to shame!"
—John Bunyan

"A few souls in any church or school or mission field may inaugurate a new condition by praying through and standing on the promises of God."
—J.A.S.

"Search and see," exclaims Bunyan. "Look in the Book and read; was there any who did trust in Him that was put to shame!"

How often I have been inspired and helped during times of persecution and discouragement in the mission field by the bright promises of Jehovah!

"A man shall be as an hiding place from the wind, and a covert from the tempest; as rivers of waters in a dry place, as the shadow of a great rock in a weary land" (Isa. 32:2).

"The Lord shall command the blessing upon thee in thy storehouses, and in all that thou settest thine hand unto; and he shall bless thee in the land which the Lord thy God giveth thee" (Deut. 28:8).

"Fear ye not, stand still, and see the salvation of the Lord, which He will shew to you to day: for the Egyptians whom ye have seen today, ye shall see them again no more for ever. The Lord shall fight for you, and ye shall hold your peace" (Exod. 14:13, 14).

"One man of you shall chase a thousand: for the Lord your God, He it is that fighteth for you, as He hath promised you" (Joshua 23:10).

"Sanctify yourselves: for to morrow the Lord will do wonders among you" (Joshua 3:5).

"Sit still, my daughter, until thou know how the matter will fall: for the man [our Kinsman Redeemer] will not be in rest, until he have finished the thing this day" (Ruth 3:18).

"For in the time of trouble he shall hide me in his pavilion: in the secret of his tabernacle shall He hide me; He shall set me up upon a rock. And now shall mine head be lifted up above mine enemies round about me: therefore will I offer in His tabernacle sacrifices of joy; I will sing, yea, I will sing praises unto the Lord" (Ps. 27:5,6).

"I am the Lord thy God, which brought thee out of the land of Egypt: open thy mouth wide, and I will fill it" (Ps. 81:10).

"And the Lord shall guide thee continually, and satisfy thy soul in drought, and make fat thy bones: and thou shalt be like a watered garden, and like a spring of water, whose waters fail not. And they that shall be of thee shall build the old waste places: thou shalt raise up the foundations of many generations; and thou shalt be called, The repairer of the breach, The restorer of paths to dwell in" (Isa. 58:11, 12).

"No weapon that is formed against thee shall prosper; and every tongue that shall rise against thee in judgment thou shalt condemn. This is the heritage of the servants of the Lord . . ." (Isa. 54:17).

"I will go before thee, and make the crooked places straight: I will break in pieces the gates of brass, and cut in sunder the bars of iron: and I will give thee the treasures of darkness, and hidden riches of secret places, that thou mayest know that I, the Lord, which call thee by thy name, am the God of Israel" (Isa. 45:2,3).

"And I will bring the blind by a way that they knew not; I will lead them in paths that they have not known: I will make darkness light before them, and crooked things straight. These things will I do unto them, and not forsake them" (Isa. 42:16).

"The Lord thy God in the midst of thee is mighty; He will save, He will rejoice over thee with joy; He will rest in His love, He will joy over thee with singing" (Lit. Heb. "rest silently over thee in love," Zeph. 3:17).

These and a host of other promises have been claimed by martyrs, prisoners, lonely discouraged believers, and weary missionaries all down the ages when they felt their feet slipping. What stories and songs have been written concerning the faithfulness of our covenant-keeping God. Millions of believers can testify with Moses: "There was not one city too strong for us: the Lord our God delivered all unto us" (Deut. 2:36).

Hudson Taylor, meditating on Ezekiel 34:26, "And I will make them and the places round about my hill a blessing; and I will cause the shower to come down in his season; there shall be showers of blessing," embraced this promise. God spoke to him through this verse, and on this text alone he predicted that God was going to do "a new thing," and he believed the Lord for the first one hundred missionaries.

James Caughey pleaded and prayed and prophesied mighty local revivals throughout England on the strength of Mark 11:24. When he arrived on the shores of Great Britain from America he quietly told evangelical Methodist leaders that God was going to do mighty things. Wherever he went he preached first on this verse, "Therefore I say unto you, What things soever ye desire, when ye pray, believe that ye receive them, and ye shall have them." Churches were revolutionized, and tens of thousands of souls were saved, among whom was William Booth, the founder of the Salvation Army. Said Caughey, "Mark 11:24 is a rich mine. What precious metal may be dug from it in experience! It may be likened to a magazine also; for it has furnished me much material of war."

Pastor Harms, of Hermannsberg, Germany, when appointed to his pastorate, felt discouraged because it seemed an impossible task given him. The church in the village was small and the testimony weak. His parish, ten miles square, was overgrown with unbelief and formalism. There was no concern among the unsaved. But as he fasted and prayed he received a mighty enduement of the Spirit, whereby he was able to receive definite promises from God's Word, definite passages of Scripture which revealed to him that the whole neighborhood would be transformed. With a little band of believers he prayed through on these promises, and very soon the desert began to blossom like a rose. Large numbers flocked to hear the Word. No year passed without new awakenings. Thousands were brought into fellowship with the Church, and so great was their depths of spirituality, and so great was their missionary spirit, that it has been said by deep mature spiritual minds that very few evangelical churches in any part of the world could equal the village church of Hermannsberg.

Jonathan Goforth, after fifteen years in China, came to the deep and painful conviction that God had something mightier to do in his life and ministry. He became restless, as he began under the Spirit's anointing an intense study of the Scriptures in relation to revival. "Every passage that had any bearing upon the price of, or the road to, the accession of power became life and breath to me," he said. After months of closet-study, he believed that God would fulfil His Word in this most difficult of mission fields. Later, at one place in Manchuria, where the Holy Spirit had descended in unusual power upon the people, the Chinese evangelist asked the missionary why he had not told them that there was going to be revival. The missionary, in deep humiliation, replied that he, himself, up to a time ago, had not known that such was possible.

The story of the Telegue Mission in India is a thrilling one. The Canadian Baptist Missionary Society had only one station, right away by itself, and so it was called "The Lone Star Mission." The missionary who labored there found himself alone because of a shortage of workers, and it was resolved by the Mission Board that instead of giving him a helper they would close down the station. Boldly and bluntly the missionary told the Board that he would carry on alone, if only to leave his bones there as a witness to Christ. Touched by his impassioned earnestness, the Board resolved to make one more attempt, and a helper was sent. The lonely laborer definitely claimed and believed, on the authority of the Word of God, that a mighty movement of the Spirit was coming. Before long their prayers were answered, and the good news was flashed back to the thousands of praying saints in North America that God had performed a miracle. As strong an authority as Dr. A. T. Pierson has left on record: "Probably the largest number of people baptized at one time since the Day of Pentecost took place at the Lone Star Mission. Two thousand two hundred and twenty-two converts were baptized in a single day!"

For seven years Adoniram Judson sought the conversion of the Burmese, and when advised by the Missionary Society to surrender his mission and start in another field he answered, "No! No! I cannot and will not surrender this mission. Success is as certain here as the promise of a faithful God can make it." Then came the Burmese blessing.

Henry Martyn once wrote: "How shall it ever be possible to convince a Hindu or a Brahmin of anything? . . . Truly, if ever I see a Hindu a real believer in the Lord Jesus I shall see something more nearly approaching the resurrection of a dead body than anything I have yet seen." But Martyn carried on in faith, believing the promises of God, and lived to see the day when God worked just this miracle among the heathen.

As I myself have waited before the Lord, I have received definite promises of revival, for different churches and different countries. The result has been a mighty quickening among the saints and the salvation of thousands of souls. Such promises given to me have been:

"Behold, I will do a new thing; now it shall spring forth; shall ye not know it? I will even make a way in the wilderness, and rivers in the desert" (Isa. 43:19).

"I will bless thee . . . thou shalt be a blessing" (Gen. 12:2).

"Sanctify yourselves: for to morrow the Lord will do wonders among you" (Jos. 3:5).

"Behold, I will make thee a new sharp threshing instrument having teeth: thou shalt thresh the mountains, and beat them small, and shall make the hills as chaff . . . When the poor and needy seek water, and there is none, and their tongue faileth for thirst, I the Lord will hear them, I the God of Israel will not forsake them. I will open rivers in high places, and fountains in the midst of the valleys: I will make the wilderness a pool of water, and the dry land springs of water" (Isa. 41:15-18).

"Call unto me, and I will answer thee, and show thee great and mighty things, which thou knowest not" (Jer. 33:3).

"Behold, I am the Lord, the God of all flesh: is there anything too hard for me?" (Jer. 32:27).

"The people that do know their God shall be strong, and do exploits" (Dan. 11:32).

"Said I not unto thee, that, if thou wouldst believe, thou shouldst see the glory of God" (John 11:40).

"And I will restore to you the years that the locust hath eaten . . . And ye shall eat in plenty, and be satisfied, and praise the name of the Lord your God, that hath dealt wondrously with you: and my people shall never be ashamed. And ye shall know that I am in the midst of Israel, and that I am the Lord your God, and none else: and My people shall never be ashamed" (Joel 2:25-27).

"And I will sanctify My great name, which was profaned among the heathen, which ye have profaned in the midst of them; and the heathen shall know that I am the Lord, saith the Lord God, and I shall be sanctified in you before their eyes" (Ezek. 36:23).

"For verily I say unto you, That whosoever shall say unto this mountain, Be thou removed, and be thou cast into the sea; and shall not doubt in his heart, but shall believe that those things which he saith shall come to pass; he shall have whatsoever he saith" (Mark 11:23).

"In the last day, that great day of the feast, Jesus stood and cried, saying, If any man thirst, let him come unto me and drink. He that believeth on me, as the scripture hath said, out of his belly shall flow rivers of living water" (John 7:37, 38).

"From this day will I bless you" (Hag. 2:19).

A few souls in any church or school or mission field may inaugurate a new condition by praying through and standing on the promises of God. My brother, my sister, if the Lord has laid it on your heart to pray for revival in your sphere of labor, go alone on your knees with the Word before God. Make sure the desire is from the Lord, so that the motive will be for the glory of His dear Name (see Daniel's prayer, Dan. 9:17-19). Then ask Him to seal to your heart some portion of His Word, according to that which He desires to do in your midst. Once you have obtained such a promise, stand on it unflinchingly until the answer comes.

*"There shall be showers of blessing:*
*This is the promise of love;*
*There shall be seasons refreshing,*
*Sent from the Saviour above.*

*There shall be showers of blessing—*
*Precious reviving again;*
*Over the hills and the valleys*
*Sound of abundance of rain.*

*There shall be showers of blessing;*
*Send them upon us, O Lord.*
*Grant to us now a refreshing;*
*Come, and now honour Thy Word.*

*There shall be showers of blessing,*
*If we but trust and obey.*
*There shall be seasons refreshing,*
*If we let God have His way.*

—El Nathan

# IX
## Preparation for Revival

"We believe, too, that as regards secret sin; i.e., sin which is known only to the individual soul and God, to confess it at the private altar is, as a rule, sufficient to insure pardon and cleansing. We say as a rule, because we have known of many, usually such as have been in places of leadership, for whom secret acknowledgment of sin has not been sufficient. Their agonized public confessions have shown plainly that for them, at least, there was only one way of relief."

—Jonathan Goforth.

There are two schools of thought concerning revival existing among our evangelical churches today. There are those who say, "I have nothing to do with the workings of God in the church: God is sovereign, and if He will send blessing, well and good, but we have no responsibility toward its coming." There are others who believe it is possible to "promote" revival in just the same way one promotes a great business enterprise, using the methods, means, and psychology of this world, and then praying God's blessings on these means. If the organization is big enough, the preacher great enough, the advertising effective enough, and the co-operation among the churches strong enough, revival is certain to be the result, as a natural matter of course.

We cannot agree with either of these attitudes toward revival. Certainly the reasoning of the first-mentioned group is wrong. God's sovereignty and man's responsibility never clash in the Word of God. In His inscrutable wisdom and providence God has chosen to do His work in the world through His saints, and has so bound up His purposes with man that He limits His workings to man's obedience. Such condescension is implied in the verse: "I will yet for this be inquired of by the house of Israel, to do it for them" (Ezek. 36:37). When Daniel understood, by the reading of the Word, the near fulfillment of God's prophecy through Jeremiah, he did not sit at ease in Zion, but immediately began to fast and to pray and to seek God's face for the full accomplishment of this prophecy.

No one has stated the truth of the Church's responsibility with greater clarity than did Charles Finney when he declared: "Revival is the result of the *right use of the appropriate* means. *The means which God has enjoined for the production of revival doubtless has a natural tendency to produce revival; otherwise God would not have enjoined them.* Means will not produce revival, we all know, without the blessing of God. No more will grain, when it is sown, produce a crop without the blessing of God. Who can say that there is not as direct an influence or agency from God to produce a crop of grain as there is to produce a revival. . . .

"On the other hand, there has long been an idea prevalent that promoting religion has something peculiar in it, not to be judged by the ordinary rules of cause and effect; in short, that there is no connection of the means with the result, and no tendency in the means to produce the effect. No doctrine is more dangerous than this to the prosperity of the Church, and nothing more absurd. Suppose a man were to go and preach this doctrine among farmers regarding their sowing of grain. Let him tell them that God is a Sovereign God and will give them a crop when it pleases Him, and that for them to plough and plant, and labor as if they expected to raise a crop, is very wrong; that it amounts to taking the work out of the hand of God, that it is interference with His sovereignty, and that there is no connection between the means and the result on which they can depend. Supposing the farmers should believe such a doctrine. Why, they would starve the world to death!

"Just such results would follow on the Church being persuaded that promoting revival is somehow so mysteriously a subject of divine sovereignty that there is no natural connection between the means and the end. In fact, what have been the results of such a doctrine in the Church? Why, generation after generation has gone to hell while the Church has been dreaming and waiting for God to save them without the use of means. This has been the devil's most successful means of destroying souls."

*If we cannot agree with the first attitude toward revival, neither can we acquiesce in the logic of the second.* Indeed, as there are strict natural laws to be observed before a natural phenomenon can take place, so there are equally definite spiritual laws which must be observed for revival to be effected. These laws are not arbitrary nor nebulous; they have their origin in the very nature of God. They are clearly outlined for us in the Holy Book. Through obedience to these spiritual laws, I believe, that they have a natural tendency to effect revival in the Church.

However, there is no relationship between God's way of promoting revival among the saints and the world's way of promoting Big Business. In fact, the two are diametrically opposed to each other, as we have seen in previous chapters.

Pastor Edward Last, of precious memory, has stated, "While the churches cannot MAKE revival, they can prepare for it, and be ready to make the most of it when it comes, and, paradoxical as it may seem, the church *that is fully prepared for revival is already in it." The* Church needs to rethink God's means of preparing for revival, as set forth for us in His Word.

IN THE FIRST PLACE, THERE MUST BE GENUINE PRAYER FOR REVIVAL. It is a solemn and awesome sight to see a company of saints on their knees, definitely seeking the face of the Lord of Hosts for a mighty awakening, crying, "Awake, awake, put on strength, O arm of the Lord; awake, as in the ancient days, in the generations of old" (Isa. 51:9). "It is time for thee, LORD, to work: for they have made void thy law" (Ps. 119:126). Surely the angels must lean over the parapets of glory and look down upon this awesome sight. But such prayer must be genuine. "Reality! Reality!" cried Duncan Matheson during times of revival in Scotland. "God must have reality!" Surely this is what our Lord meant when He said to His disciples, "When thou prayest, thou shalt not be as the *hypocrites.* The word "hypocrite" primarily means "a play actor," "one who acts a part." "When you pray do not wear a mask." It was the custom for Greek and Roman actors to speak in large masks with mechanical devices for augmenting the force of the voice. The hypocrite or play actor must have an audience before whom he will play his part and who will applaud his deed well done. It is said that when a well-known clergyman prayed once at a celebration at Bunker Hill, in Boston, a newspaper reported next day that "the Reverend prayed the most eloquent prayer ever addressed to a Boston audience!" Certainly prayer is not talking to man, but talking to God, who sees through all our pretence.

PRAYER, TO BE GENUINE AND REAL, MUST HAVE A PURE MOTIVE. When Brownlow North, who was later so mightily used of God in the 1859 revival in Scotland, once asked the godly Duchess Elizabeth of Gordon, "Duchess, what should a man do who has often prayed to God and who has never been answered?," the duchess quietly made reply in the words of James 4:3, "Ye ask, and receive not, because ye ask amiss." The duchess, upon writing later of this incident, said, "At this his countenance changed. He became very greatly moved, was very quiet during the evening, and thanked me ere he left." *Any prayer for revival which does not have for its motive the glory of God, and only the glory of God, is prayer that "asks amiss."*

The majority of prayers for revival are carnal and selfish. Some want revival for the glory of their own denomination, and if God sent blessing to a church other than their own they

122

would be offended before the Lord (Matt. 13:57). I remember as a boy how, in Glasgow, we were on the verge of a mighty spiritual awakening for the whole city, the largest in Scotland. All-night prayer meetings were held, and expectation ran high that God was going to do a "new thing." The believers sang in great faith to the early hours of the morning:

> *In this dear land, in days of yore,*
> *God moved in mighty power.*
> *His Word He blessed, and souls found rest*
> *When Scotland was on fire.*

> *Once more, Lord, once more,*
> *As in the days of yore,*
> *On this dear land Thy Spirit pour;*
> *Set Scotland now on fire!*

God answered the believing prayers of His people, and a spontaneous awakening took place, not in a big city church, but in a mission hall in the small mining town of Lambhill, on the outskirts of the city. My spiritual father, Mr. Tom Rea of Belfast, was leading the saints there in a prayer crusade, asking God to rend the heavens and visit them. The presence of the Lord was felt everywhere, in the shops, in the homes, and even under the bowels of the earth where many miners were smitten by the Holy Spirit. Meetings went on for many weeks night after night. Mr. Rea invited me to come down and help in dealing with anxious souls. It was an astonishing sight to me. It was impossible for us to leave the hall before midnight, owing to the deep distress among anxious souls. It was Brother Rea's burden that the fire of God would spread to the city, which at that time was the greatest evangelical city in the world. We prayed together to this effect, but alas, we soon discovered that the evangelical leaders of the city were offended at the Lord that the revival had not begun in one of their great congregations. In looking back now over a period of some thirty-three years I am sincerely persuaded that the revival fires would have spread into the whole city and possibly to the whole nation had these evangelical leaders at that time not dictated to God as to where the revival should begin.

In contrast, when speaking with a Bishop of the Lutheran Church in Europe, in later years, at the beginning of a great awakening in his land, he said to us, "I do not care, Mr. Stewart, where the fire of God falls, whether it is in the Cathedral or in the Salvation Army Hall, for one thing I know, you cannot keep revival to yourself. If one group tries to control the fire of God it will burn them." Can you wonder that this dear man of God saw the blessing of revival in his church?

In praying for revival, there must not only be purity of motive, but THERE MUST BE UNITY OF DESIRE AND PURPOSE. On the Day of Pentecost, we read, "These all continued with one accord in prayer and supplication . . . they were all with one accord in one place" (Acts 1:14; 2:1).

> He found them in His house of prayer,
>     With one accord assembled,
> And so revealed His presence there,
>     They wept for joy, and trembled.
> One cup they drank, one bread they break,
>     One baptism shared, and language spake,
> Forgiving and forgiven.
>     Then forth they went with tongues of flame,
> In one blest theme delighting,
>     The Love of Jesus and His Name
> God's children all uniting.

*That love our theme and watchword still,*
*The law of love may we fulfil,*
*And love as we are loved.*

—A Moravian Hymn

A Nineteenth Century revivalist wrote: "Suppose a church should undertake to pray for revival, and should all be agreed in desiring revival, but not as to the *time when* it shall be. Suppose some wished to have the revival come now and are prepared with their hearts, waiting for the Spirit of God to come down and are willing to give time and attention and labor to it NOW, but others are not quite ready, as they have something else to attend to at present; some worldly object which they want to accomplish, some piece of business in hand, wanting just to finish this thing, and then they would have the revival come. They cannot possibly find time to attend to it NOW; they are not prepared to humble themselves, to search their hearts, and break up their fallow ground, and put themselves in a posture to receive the blessing. Is it not plain that there is no real union, for they are not agreed in that which is essential! While some are praying that revival may come NOW, others are praying with equal earnestness that it may NOT.

"Suppose the question were put to THIS church, 'Are you agreed in praying for revival here? Do you all desire revival, and would you all like to have it NOW? Would you be heartily agreed NOW to break down in the dust and open your hearts to the Holy Ghost if He should come tonight?' I do not ask what you would say, if I should propose the question. Perhaps if I should put it now you would all rise up and VOTE, that you are agreed in desiring revival and agreed in having it NOW. You know how you ought to feel and what you ought to say, and you know that you ought to be ready for revival,

NOW. But I ask you, 'Would God see it to be so in your hearts, that you are agreed on this point, and praying accordingly?' If not, when will you be agreed to pray for revival? *And if this church cannot be agreed among themselves, how can you expect revival?* It is of no use for you to stand up here and say you are agreed when God reads the heart and sees that you are not agreed. Here is the promise: 'Again I say unto you, That if two of you shall agree on earth as touching any thing that they shall ask, it shall be done for them of my Father which is in heaven' (Matt. 18:19). Now, this is either true or false. Which ground will you take? If it is true, then it is true that you are not agreed and never have been, except in those cases when you have had revival.

"But we must agree not only on A time, but it must be the PRESENT time, or we are not agreed on everything essential to the work. Unless we agree to have revival NOW, we shall not NOW use the means, and until the means are used it cannot come. It is plain, then, that we must be agreed on the present time; that is, we are not agreed in the sense of the text, until we are agreed that NOW we will have the blessing, and act accordingly. To agree on a future time is no use, for when that future time comes, we must *then* be agreed upon *that present time, and use* means accordingly, so that you see you are never properly agreed until you agree that NOW is the time."

God is ready and longing to send revival. "Call unto me and I will answer thee, and show thee great and mighty things which thou knowest not," is His challenge to us today. It is true that we must wait God's time for revival, and cannot force it; but is it not also true that *HIS time is when* the *Church is prepared for the blessing?* There is nothing fluctuating or spasmodic about God's desires for His people. Their UN-

126

PREPAREDNESS is the only problem. The Church might have revival as wide and as deep and as powerful as she please, if she would only comply with the conditions on which God can grant it.

One of the most important things to observe in our Christian life and service is the CONDITION attached to any blessing that we may need. "Make this valley full of ditches" was the word of the Lord through the prophet Elijah to the King of Israel (2 Kings 3:16). And after they had made the ditches, the Lord caused the water to come and fill them. In like manner, when there is obedience on our part to the divine condition, there follows abundant blessing and continuous victory. The depth of the ditch shows the measure of the expected blessing.

The great Moravian Pentecost was not a shower of blessing out of a cloudless sky. It did come suddenly—as suddenly as the blessing of its greater predecessor in Jerusalem, when the Christian Church was born. Yet for long years there had been signs of abundance of rain, though many did not recognize them. In short, the blessing of the 13th of August 1727 was diligently and earnestly prepared for. We know of no annals in Church history which evidenced greater desire for the outpouring of the Holy Spirit, and more patient and persistent efforts in that direction, than those of the Moravian Church between the years 1725 and 1737. The Church *must once again begin to dig* her *ditches.*

TRUE ACKNOWLEDGMENT AND CONFESSION OF SIN is, as it were, "making the ditches." There are times when we must stop praying for revival and get up from our knees and deal with the sin in our midst. In Joshua, chapter 7, we see typified a group of believers praying for revival, without having first "made the ditches." They are blaming God for failing to answer prayer in this respect. Joshua, baffled and beaten in disgrace because of the defeat at Ai, "rent his clothes, and fell to the earth upon his face before the ark of the Lord until eventide, he and the elders of Israel, and put dust upon their heads. And Joshua said, Alas, O Lord God, wherefore hast Thou at all brought this people over Jordan, to deliver us into the hands of the Amorites, to destroy us? Would to God we had been content, and dwelt on the other side Jordan! O Lord, what shall I say, when Israel turneth their backs before their enemies! For the Canaanites and all the inhabitants of the land shall hear of it, and shall environ us round, and cut off our name from the earth: and what wilt Thou do unto Thy Great Name?" (vv. 6-9). Joshua insinuated that Jehovah was not interested in taking care of His own Name—that the cause of defeat and failure was that God would not hear and answer prayer. The Lord's rebuke to His servant was sharp and sure: "Get thee up: wherefore liest thou thus upon thy face? IS-RAEL HATH SINNED." How many times God must say to believers praying for revival:"Get thee up, wherefore liest thou thus upon thy face? There is SIN in the camp."

Joshua could have wasted all his energies in order to win the victory at Ai, but all would have been in vain so long as Achan's sin was not judged in the midst of God's ancient people. Even so, there are times in the experience of the Church of God when one has to cease preaching or even praying or exhibiting the Table of Commandments; when one has indeed to "grab at the golden calf" and smash it and scatter it to the four winds. No wonder Douglas Brown, in revival times, declared, "Revival is not going down the street beating big drums, but believers with sobbing hearts going back to Calvary."

Let no one begin to pray for revival who cannot first honestly and sincerely face this fundamental condition. The very first act of obedience to God of any human being must consist of repentance and breaking with every known sin. Breaking with sin means breaking with any bad habit, with any mode of life, with any practice or even any attitude which dishonors the Lord. Sin must immediately be judged and dealt with, lest leprosy spread abroad in the camp. God's message for us today is:"Up, sanctify the people" (Joshua 7:13). An Achan in the camp can hinder God from blessing—an Achan of doubt, an Achan of worldliness, an Achan of selfishness, an Achan of jealousy, an Achan of pride, an Achan of covetousness, an Achan of impurity. GOD WILL NOT ALLOW HIS NAME TO BE ASSOCIATED WITH SIN. God's name was too holy for Him to be associated with any evil, and so He was not in their midst.

In Joshua 3:5 we have the challenge from God, "Sanctify yourselves, for to morrow the Lord will do wonders among you." This clarion call of God was sounded throughout the camp of Israel on the eve of the memorial day, when after forty years of wilderness failure they crossed over Jordan into the Promised Land. The law which underlies this command is an eternal one. *Every mighty movement of the Holy Spirit is preceded by a preparation of heart among God's people.* God's tomorrow of wonders waits for our today of sanctification, God does not need any preparation. He is always ready, always ready to work wonders. Prayer is neither preparing God nor making God willing to work wonders. Prayer is the preparation of the heart of the one who prays, for the wonders which God is waiting to do for him. Upon us rests the responsibility of fixing the time of God's display of power, for there is no delay with Him. The "might of His power is constant and unchanging, but the supernatural workings vary according to the receptiveness and obedience of His people."

"Sanctify yourselves!" The word "sanctify" in this verse simply means, "put yourself in that attitude or position where

129

God can with perfect readiness work for you." It is only when the river of God approaches human territory that it is stopped or hindered. The windows that hold back the mighty blessing are bolted on our side and not on God's. If we will pull back the bolts of unquestioning obedience, our "today of sanctification" will be followed by "God's tomorrow of wonders."

> *Oh for the floods on the thirsty land,*
> *Oh for a mighty revival!*
> *Oh for a sanctified, fearless band*
> *Ready to hail its arrival!*

# X
# Prayer Which Brings Revival

"If every true pastor, evangelist, and missionary throughout the world would simultaneously turn unto God in utter
self-humbling, in intercession, in seeking the face of God and
in repentance, such an upheaval of holy prayer would shake
the world."

—D. M. PANTON.

"The need of the hour is for intercessors in vital union
with their ascended Lord, to agonize inside the veil for deliverance of the church from its spiritual slump."

—J.A.S.

The need of the hour is for definite, prevailing, agonizing prayer for God to rend the heavens and visit His blood-bought people. Dr. R. A. Torrey has stated, "Doubtless one of the great secrets of the unsatisfactoriness and superficiality and unreality of many of our modern so-called 'revivals' is that more dependence is put upon man's machinery rather than upon God's power, sought and obtained by earnest, persistent, believing prayer." We live in a day characterized by the multiplication of man's machinery and the diminution of God's power. The great cry of our day is "Work, work, work! New organizations, new methods, new machinery." The great *need* of our *day* is *prayer.* It was a master-stroke of the devil when he got the Church to generally lay aside this mighty weapon of prayer. The devil is perfectly willing that the Church should multiply its organization, and deftly-contrived machinery for the conquest of the world for Christ, if it will only give up praying.

Whenever you see revival in any place, if you will inquire among the members of the church or churches you will find that an unknown Jacob has been wrestling in prayer for the blessing; some Elijah, alone perhaps, with head bowed between his knees, has been praying for a spiritual deluge, and keeping a sharp lookout for the gathering clouds. The Lord cried through Ezekiel in his day, "And I sought for a man among them, that should make up the hedge, and stand in the gap before me for the land . . . but I found none (Ezek.

22:30). And in our day the cry is the same; *there is a great need for more intercessors in vital union with their ascended Lord, who will agonize inside the veil for the deliverance of the Church from its spiritual "slump."*

In Acts 12:5 we read that "prayer was made without ceasing of the church unto God" for Peter in prison. The word translated "without ceasing" literally means "stretched-out-ed-ly," suggesting the intensity with which the church stretched out toward God in agonizing desire for Peter's deliverance. Here we have a picture of spiritual travail among the saints for the deliverance of a brother. This is the kind of prayer that prevails with God, and brings forth response that amazes even those who are praying! Much of our modern prayers have no power in them because there is no heart in them. They lack intenseness and fervor.

*True prayer is an aggressive, unseen, closet ministry in co-operation with the Holy Spirit, for the purpose of dislodging the powers of darkness from the strategic position which they occupy in the Church and in the world.* This kind of prayer brings God into the battle. "For the weapons of our warfare," says Paul, "are . . . mighty through God to the pulling down of strong holds" (2 Cor. 10:4). Prayer is the Christian's secret weapon. The clarion call is for believers everywhere to "stand in the gap" and, linked with the triumphant Christ through the victory of Calvary, to bring to bear an aggressive warfare against the satanic forces.

The demons of hell are real, and Satan, the great archenemy of the Church, is seeking to "wear out the saints." We must recognize that it is Satan who has blinded the minds of the saints and kept them in ignorance of their birthright privileges and of their responsibility to live an overcoming life by the power of the Holy Spirit. It is he who, through worldliness, has caused them to leave their first love. It is he who seeks to hinder revival among the saints of God today. Therefore, as we pray for revival, we must not only resist our foe in the all-conquering name of the Lord Jesus, but we must proceed to drive him off the field through that same glorious Name. This we have been given the power to do through Him who "spoiled principalities and powers," who "made a shew of them openly, triumphing over them in it" (Col. 2:15).

The early Church knew the secret of overcoming through this glorious weapon of prayer. As wave after wave of satanic opposition broke over them, they conquered on their knees. They went forward on their knees. They lived at the Throne. The need in the Church today is to rediscover the secret of power to wrestle with God like Paul and the spirit to agonize in prayer like Epaphras. Then, through our union with Christ on the Cross, prayer will be filled with the Spirit of conquest through which we will be able to vanquish the foe and shout the victory over him. It is not enough that we "resist the devil," who seeks to deceive and to divide the saints of the Lord, thus bringing impotence upon a subnormal church. The Word of God teaches us that we must be "more than conquerors" in the conquest.

"Whatsoever thou shalt bind on earth shall be bound in heaven: and whatsoever thou shalt loose on earth shall be loosed in heaven" (Matt. 16:19).

"Elias was a man subject to like passions as we are, and he prayed earnestly that it might not rain: and it rained not on the earth by the space of three years and six months. And he prayed again, and the heaven gave rain" (Jas. 5:17-18).

"Through thee will we push down our enemies: through thy name will we tread them under that rise up against us" (Ps. 44:5).

"How can one enter into a strong man's house, and spoil his goods, except he first bind the strong man? and then he will spoil his house" (Matt. 12:29).

"I will rebuke the devourer for your sakes, and he shall not destroy" (Mal. 3:11).

Ephesians 6 portrays to us the battle arena with the battle drawn, and no quarter given to the enemy. In verses 12, 13 and 18 we read, "For we wrestle not against flesh and blood, but against principalities, against powers, against the rulers of the darkness of this world, against spiritual wickedness in high places. Wherefore take unto you the whole armour of God, that ye may be able to withstand in the evil day, and having done all, to stand. . . . Praying always with all prayer and supplication in the Spirit, and watching thereunto with all perseverance and supplication for all saints."

The victorious intercessor, having vanquished the foe on the battlefield, must remain standing for further conquests, using the shield of faith, and wielding the sword of the Spirit. The prayer warrior goes on conquering and to conquer, standing on the ground of Christ's victory.

In the Authorized Version the admonition "watching thereunto" literally means "being sleepless thereunto." The intercessor must be alert and keep alert. He is persistent in earnest, unceasing intercession for the saints. Paul beseeches the saints in Rome to "strive" together with him in prayer. The word "strive" means primarily to contend as a warrior in a fight. The same thought is brought out in the mighty ministry of Epaphras: "Who is . . . always labouring fervently for you in prayers" (Col. 4:12). Such earnestness in prayer is illustrated graphically for us in the Garden of Gethsemane where our blessed Lord's "sweat was as it were great drops of blood" (Luke 22:44). We are told that our Saviour was in great agony and "STILL He prayed more earnestly." Oh, how cold and indifferent are our own prayers in comparison! Our Lord, in the Parable of Importunity, in Luke 11:8, teaches us the same lesson of persistent, earnest asking. "Yet because of his importunity he will rise and give him as many as he needeth." The word translated "importunity" is a very striking one, used only here in the New Testament. It means literally "barefacedness" or "shamelessness." The man of the parable was shameless in the boldness of his asking. He was shameless in awakening his neighbor at the midnight hour. He was shameless because he was desperate in his plight; he had no bread to set before his guest!

*I have discovered in my own revival ministry that God only answers the prayers of the saints who are desperate.* How many are praying for revival who are not burdened and broken? Hannah is set forth in the Word as a desperate believer praying for revival (1 Sam. 1). Nothing mattered in her life but that God would answer her prayer and give her a son. She was a heart-broken woman. So great was her agony that she could not speak, but could only weep. Even the high priest of God misunderstood her condition and thought she was drunk, as she went into the house of God to agonize. Hear the words of the burdened saint: "No, my lord, I am a woman of a sorrowful spirit: I have drunk neither wine nor strong drink, but have poured out my soul before the Lord" (v. 15). The reason why we have so few revivals is that we have so few desperate believers who are willing to pay the price of this closet ministry.

Mr. Finney tells of a poor consumptive who was unable to do anything more than pray. Yet so mighty was he in intercession that revivals sprang up as if spontaneously and unaccountably. After his death his diary revealed the secret behind these great blessings.

John Knox was a man so famous for his power in prayer that "Bloody Queen Mary" used to say that she feared his prayers more than all the mighty armies in Europe. He was often in such agony for the deliverance of his country that he could not sleep. "Lord, give me Scotland, or I die" was the cry constantly on the lips of the Reformer. So mightily did God hear his cry that "The Land of the Heather" became the most fruitful vineyard in the entire world.

The good John Welsh of Ayr felt that his day was ill-spent if he did not spend at least seven or eight hours in prayers. On going to rest, he used to lay a plaid on top of the bedclothes so that when he arose for his night prayers he might cover himself in the cold room. Sometimes he would retire to the church, which was a little distance from the town, and there pray all the night through.

One of the heart-touching incidents of Scottish history is the glorious closet-work of William C. Burns. He prayed for hours daily as he began his public ministry at the age of twenty. One morning, when his mother came to his bedroom to call him to his breakfast, she found him lying on the floor where he had been detained by the Spirit all night in mighty pleadings. He greeted her with the words, "Mother, God has given me Scotland today!" In a short time the whole of Scotland was shaken by a mighty spiritual upheaval without any organized effort.

In Newport, Wales, there was a prayer circle of praying men who met together every Saturday night for over thirty years to pray for blessing. Not one death occurred in the circle during this time. They began to pray, in the first place, because they felt burdened that Charles Spurgeon needed a mighty anointing as he was beginning his ministry in London. It is very remarkable to notice that on the very Lord's day following the first prayer meeting Spurgeon began to preach with such increased unction that it was noticeable to all.

*To our sorrow, we have discovered many pastors and churches praying for the revival who will never see the answer to their prayers, because their church is not geared to the scriptural pattern of revival.* Their program is not that of the Spirit. There is no preparation for revival. There is no mighty upsurge of intercession. They are evangelical and orthodox. They live a quiet, consistent Christian testimony, but something is sadly lacking. There is no desperation over the sinful conditions of a subnormal church. They know nothing of vital intercession, such as characterized the life of Elijah, whose "energized prayer was of great force."

Many times I have gone to a fine church for meetings, only to discover that, although the members loved the Lord and His Word, there was no sign of revival. There were no souls being saved. There was no outreaching to the ends of the earth with a deep foreign mission enterprise. The reason was not far to seek. These people did not know the joy of holy travail on behalf of a sleeping Church and dying world. They spent many hours studying their Bibles, but spent very little time at the Throne. I found that there were no moral sins that kept back the blessing. It was the coldness and complacency of their own hearts. They sat at ease in Zion, with no passion for souls. When the Spirit broke them down, and filled their hearts with the fire of Christ's love, and poured out upon them the spirit of agony and intercession for the salvation of those about them, then revival came into their midst. Oh, how alarming is the condition of the evangelical Church today! How few churches have one real, desperate prayer meeting a week. We oftentimes sing, "A little talk with Jesus makes it quite all right," but, beloved, it is going to take more than a little talk with Jesus to bring revival. If, as our Lord said, it takes extraordinary prayer and fasting to cast out one demon from one person, how much less can we expect to have him cast out of the Church and the world without any?

During "The Great Awakening," Jonathan Edwards wrote with great logic: "Why should it be thought strange that those who are full of the Spirit of Christ should be proportionately in their souls like to Christ, who had so strong a love for them and concern for them as to be willing to drink the dregs of the cup of God's fury for them; and at the same time, as their High Priest, offer up strong crying and tears with extreme agony when He was in travail for their souls? The spirit of those that have been in distress for the souls of others in this revival, so far as I can discern, seems not to be different from that of the apostle, who travailed for souls, and was ready to wish himself accursed from Christ for others."

*There has never been a true awakening anywhere on earth until there was a desperate Church.* It is when we are in desperation that God steps in and answers our prayers mightily. I knew a business man, a wealthy, influential manufacturer, who was so burdened for the spiritual condition of his country that he arose every morning at five o'clock to seek the face of the Lord for this matter. For years he prayed on in faith, until the answer came. He prayed that God would raise up other believers with like minds to join him all over the land in this secret ministry. So desperate was he that he told the Lord that if he would send revival, he would spend his entire wealth for the evangelization of the nation. This dear brother kept his word, as he became the human center of the revival movement in his land.

I knew a local church in an Eastern European land which, because of coldness, had only some twenty believers gathering on Sunday night for Bible study. Some suggested that they close the building and give up their testimony in that predominantly Roman Catholic city. A few held on in faith and, with careful deliberation, being elderly people, had a solemn meeting of dedication where they told God that whatever should be the price for an awakening in their church and city they were willing to pay it. After bringing all their tithes to God's storehouse, and laying themselves on the altar, they continued for many months seeking the face of the Lord. It was the biggest thing in their life. It was the one thing that crowded their horizons. It was the theme of their talk at all times. They were brothers and sisters with a purpose. They would not let go of the Lord until He had blessed them. When I began meetings in their church, many hundreds of souls were saved from the opening nights, many among them being the children of those who had been praying. So mightily did the Lord work in the church to the salvation of souls that very soon the building which seated some eight hundred people was packed to capacity at every meeting. Without any pastor, they soon overflowed their banks, so that some twenty mission stations were established in Roman Catholic districts around them. This place became the mother church to many groups of believers. From this church the members went forth all over their country evangelizing. The deadest church in the nation became the most spiritual and wide-awake. When the Spirit of God began to work at the beginning, so great was the power of Jehovah that they carried on meetings every night for many months. These meetings were necessary because of the power of the Spirit resting upon the young converts, who in turn were winning others for the Lord. The elderly saints who had waited before the Lord now had the joy of building up the young converts in the most holy faith.

In another country in Europe, when a bishop thanked me for the revival which had taken place in his denomination during the course of several years, in which his own life was greatly influenced, I told him that the awakening came to his church not through my preaching but I believe because of the burden of one lone woman. This sister, the wife of a nobleman, had to my mind the greatest spirit of intercession and agony of any believer in the country. I found her in the different churches at all hours of the day or night where prayer meetings were being held. On one occasion, when she had been praying in a Methodist church for several hours, I spoke to her around three o'clock in the morning, quietly suggesting that she had been praying long hours and it would be good if she went home to rest. She replied through her tears, "Brother James, I cannot rest at home until God does a new thing for the spiritual life of my denomination." No wonder that later her husband's life was revolutionized during the revival and he became the mightiest evangelist of the nation!

Oh, that every reader might be willing to pay the price for revival blessing! With deep spiritual insight Mrs. Booth-Clibborn (The Maréchale) wrote:

### CRUCIFIED

*There is no gain but by a loss.*
*We cannot save but by the cross.*
*The corn of wheat, to multiply,*
*Must fall into the ground and die.*
*Oh, should a soul alone remain,*
*When it a hundredfold can gain?*

*Our souls are held by all they hold.*
*Slaves still are slaves in chains of gold,*
*To whatsoever we may cling*
*We make it a soul-chaining thing.*
*Whether it be a life or land*
*Or dear as our right eye or hand.*

142

*Wherever we ripe fields behold*
*Waving to God their sheaves of gold,*
*Be sure some corn of wheat has died;*
*Some saintly soul been crucified;*
*Someone has suffered, wept and prayed,*
*And fought hell's legions undismayed.*

—by Mrs. Booth-Clibborn

# XI

# Worldliness and Revival

"I looked for the Church and I found it in the world; I looked for the world, and alas, I found it in the Church."
—Andrew Bonar

"Worldliness is an atmosphere in which one lives and which robs the Christian life of its radiant, dynamic character."
—J.A.S.

From the broken heart of Jehovah comes the scathing rebuke to His people: "For my people have committed two evils; they have forsaken me the fountain of living waters, and hewed them out cisterns, broken cisterns, that can hold no water" (Jer. 2:13).

Today how many believers have forsaken the Lord Jesus, the Fountain of all true satisfaction and heart-rest, and are seeking joy in worldly pleasures! They profess to love Him and serve Him, and yet they have allowed the attractions of this world to dim their spiritual eyesight. Worldliness robs the Christian life of its vital, radiant, dynamic character. Worldliness is anything that takes the keen edge off my spiritual life and dims my vision of the Lord. Worldliness is anything that robs me of my deep inner love-life with my glorious Redeemer. Worldliness is anything that takes away my burden for souls. Worldliness is anything that hinders my spending time in the closet in earnest intercession, by the power of the Spirit, for the Church and the world.

> *Whatever passes as a cloud between*
> *The mental eye of faith and things unseen,*
> *Causing that brighter world to disappear,*
> *Or seem less lovely, or its hope less dear;*
> *THAT is our world—our idol, though it bear*
> *Affection's impress or devotion's air.*

*The curse of worldliness has invaded the Church. We must enter a crusade against it.* We cannot be neutral. We cannot be silent. It is a matter of life and death. The Church is slowly being choked to death in the atmosphere of worldliness. Worldliness robs the Church of its purity and power, and places her in a position where she cannot be a true bride of the Lord. It places her in a position where she cannot proclaim the whole counsel of God. In the study of church history we find that the pilgrim church never had so much power over the world as when she had nothing to do with it!

The end times are upon us, and Satan is employing every means possible to crowd the Lord out of the lives of His saints. He is finding very effective, for instance, his scheme of invading their homes through the medium of the television.

The vast majority of evangelicals who would not for one moment visit places of worldly amusement allow the same places to enter their homes through the medium of television. The popular programs have more power over many of God's children than the weeknight prayer meetings. Many "television Christians" know better the names of current film stars, comedians, sportsmen and politicians than they know the names and characters of the Bible.

*There is an established pattern that has settled in our evangelical churches all over the North American Continent.* The majority of members attend the service on Sunday morning. Less than fifty per cent attend the evening Gospel service. Less than twenty per cent attend the only weeknight praying meeting of the assembly. Thousands of hours each year are forever lost over worldly television programs, which should have been spent in deep spiritual conversation, study of the Word, and glorious communion with the Lord. Surely the hardest and most discouraging task on earth today is to be assigned by the Head of the Church to shepherd such flocks.

I had far rather face a Soviet firing squad than to be the pastor of such a people. I had rather spend five years in a Soviet prison camp than five years as pastor of some of these churches! We know of one pastor who could not understand why his prayers for revival in his church were not being answered, even though he and his wife fasted and prayed far into the night. One Sunday, on his way to the prayer meeting before the evening service, he visited some of his best members, who had not been present in the service that morning. He feared they were ill. Imagine his dismay and astonishment when he discovered that they and four other church families had settled down for the evening around a worldly television show. We know of another pastor who went a great distance to visit some of his members in order to read and pray with them, as is the custom with every holy man of God. They welcomed him and served him coffee, but gave him no time to talk with them about the Lord. They had their favorite television program on and did not offer to turn it off during the whole visit. There was no opportunity for spiritual conversation, and the pastor left with a terrible sense of frustration. The tragedy was that these dear evangelicals felt no sense of shame that they had allowed a program to crowd out the Lord that day, as such action was their normal daily routine.

If Andrew Bonar could say seventy years ago: "I looked for the Church and I found it in the world; I looked for the world, and alas, I found it in the Church!" what would this dear man of God say to us today? When I see these starry-eyed evangelical television fans wasting precious hours that could be spent more profitably, the words of Paul to the Galatians keep coming to my mind, "O foolish Galatians, who hath bewitched you, that ye should not obey the truth, before whose eyes Jesus Christ hath been evidently set forth, cruci-

149

fied among you?" (Gal. 3:1). Who has been casting a spell over you? Surely today it is Satan, through the eye-gate!

We can easily understand how revival came among the Methodists in Britain when they sang lustily with Charles Wesley:

> *Vain delusive world, adieu,*
> *With all of creature good.*
> *Only Jesus I pursue*
> *Who bought me with His blood.*
> *All thy pleasures I forgo,*
> *I trample on thy wealth and pride,*
> *Only Jesus would I know,*
> *And Jesus crucified.*

*This worldliness dims the vision of the saints and causes them to lose the sense of eternal values.* They become eccentric in the sight of God and the holy angels. They forget that they have been purchased to be possessed. They have lost their pilgrim status. There is no longer a distinction between them and the worldlings. They no longer live as aliens and exiles. Although they profess to the unsaved that they are "strangers and pilgrims," people in a strange land, and on their way home to "The Celestial City," alas, the world does not believe them. Like Lot of old, they have lost their testimony.

*Again, because the spirit of worldliness has invaded the Church, there is so little sacrifice in the average Christian life.* The church is too comfortable and cozy. "Moab hath been at ease from his youth, and he has settled on his lees" (Jer. 48:11). Each pastor knows he has two congregations; the congregation of "the dead" and the congregation of "the living." Like Gideon, we need to have a revival by subtraction. No wonder the early Methodists had revival. John Wesley gives us the secret in a diary entry: "Visited a Society today. It had thirty-two members: stroked off twenty. Glory to God!"

*If Christians were half as much excited about their heavenly heritage as they are their earthly possessions they would be branded at once as fanatics.* Amy Carmichael wrote, "We who follow the Crucified are not here to make a pleasant thing of life; we are called to suffer for the sake of a suffering sinful world. The Lord forgive us our shameful evasions and hesitations. His brow was crowned with thorns; do we seek rosebuds for our crowning? His hands were pierced with nails; are our hands ringed with jewels? His feet were bare and bound; do our feet walk delicately? What do we know of travail? Of tears that scald before they fall? Of heartbreak? Of being scorned? God forgive us our love of ease! God forgive us that so often we turn our face from life that is even remotely like His. Forgive us that we all but worship comfort, the delight of the presence of loved ones, possessions, treasures on earth. Far, far from our prayers too often is any thought of prayer for a love which will lead us to give one whom we love; to follow our Lord to Gethsemane, to Calvary—perhaps because we have never been there ourselves."

> *From subtle love of softening things,*
> *From easy choices, weakenings*
> *(Not thus are spirits fortified,*
> *Not this way went the Crucified),*
> *From all that dims Thy Calvary,*
> *O Lamb of God, deliver me!*
>
> —Amy Carmichael

*The love of the things of this world robs the Church of her passion for souls.* Few church members take more than ca-

151

sual interest in the salvation of souls. Many of us have ceased to be amazed at the indifference without because there is so much apathy within. When I see a vacant seat in the prayer meeting I say to myself, "There is a vote against revival." When I see an empty place in the Gospel service on the Lord's Day evening I say to myself, "There is a vote against revival." When I see a Sunday School class left without a teacher I say to myself, "There is a vote against revival." When I hear of church members who leave the place of prayer for places of amusement I count up so many votes against the Lord's coming in revival power among us.

My friend, Hyman Appelman, tells the following story: "One of my truly great preacher friends relates an incident in one of his campaigns somewhere in Oklahoma. He had tried earnestly to get the church people to visit, to invite the lost to the services, but very few responded. Then came the week's half-holiday. A barber in that town, with several of his friends, went on a fishing trip. The boat overturned, drowning the barber. Everything in that town stopped as the lake was searched for the body. They hired a diver at $100.00 per day. On the fourth day the body was located. As the people slowly walked past the open coffin in the church, the pastor was heard to say softly, 'Oh, Sam, if these people had cared as much for your soul as they did for your dead body you wouldn't be in hell now!' How true! How tragically, bitterly true!"

*The Church of God must robe herself in sackcloth.* The Church of God must make a public confession of her awful position of backsliding. For a Christian redeemed by Calvary's blood to live a worldly life is treason and spiritual suicide. It is better to be poor with Philadelphia than to become rich with Laodicea.

It is better to be branded a fanatic than to be at ease in Zion.

"Go a little deeper," said a French soldier at Austerlitz, to the surgeon who was probing his left side for a bullet. "Go a little deeper, and you will find the Emperor." Oh that this were true with every child of God! Oh that we all could say with Paul: "For me to live is Christ." The love of Christ overwhelms and overmasters me! I have only one purpose in life and that is to live for the One who died, rose again, ascended, and is coming back for me! The greatest calling of every Christian is to live abundantly, actively, aggressively, joyfully, NOW, in the power of the Holy Spirit.

*Let me love Thee, Thou are claiming*
　　*Every feeling of my soul;*
*Let me love, in power prevailing,*
　　*Render Thee my life, my all;*
*For life's burdens they are easy,*
　　*And life's sorrows lose their sting*
*If they're carried, Lord, to please Thee,*
　　*If they're done Thy smile to win.*

*Let me love Thee—come revealing*
　　*All Thy love has done for me;*
*Help my doubt, so unbelieving*
　　*By the sight of Calvary;*
*Let me see Thy love despising*
　　*All the shame my sins have brought,*
*By Thy torment realizing*
　　*What a price my burden bought.*

*Let me love Thee, love is mighty,*
　　*Swaying realms of deed and thought,*
*By which I shall walk uprightly*
　　*And shall serve Thee as I ought.*
*Love will soften every sorrow,*

*Love will lighten every care,*
*Love unquestioning will follow,*
*Love will triumph, love will bear.*

Chorus:
*Let me love Thee, Saviour*
*Take my heart forever,*
*Nothing but Thy favour, Lord,*
*My soul can satisfy!*

—Wm. Booth-Clibborn

# XII
## The Holy Spirit and Revival

"There are even now seasons of extraordinary communion with the Lord when, through the Holy Spirit, He is pleased to manifest Himself to the soul in such unwonted power that they may be truly called 'times of refreshing'."

—A. J. Gordon.

"There can be no revival apart from the Holy Ghost; He is the author of every Heaven-sent movement."

—J.A.S.

There can be no revival apart from the Holy Spirit. He is the author of every heaven-sent movement. There can be no quickening to abundant life among the saints, or spiritual resurrection of the unsaved, apart from the supernatural work of the Executive Member of the Godhead. So, in seeking the Father's face for revival, we must honor and obey this blessed Comforter, Who is the Administrator of the affairs of the Church.

*In the pages of the New Testament we see that every grace of the Christian life is attributed to the indwelling power of an ungrieved Spirit.* The Holy Spirit is the One who glorifies the Lord Jesus in the experience of every child of God. The Saviour predicted, "When the Comforter is come, whom I will send unto you from the Father . . . he shall testify of me" (John 15:26). It is the whole work of the Comforter to bear witness of Christ, to reveal Christ, and to glorify Christ in our experience. We will never really know Him except by direct revelation of the Spirit. We may listen at conventions, to others speaking about Him, but unless the Heavenly Teacher Himself interprets and applies the message of God to our own souls we can never really know Christ.

*Not only does the Spirit reveal Christ, but He also forms the indwelling Christ in our hearts and minds.* Our Redeemer promised in His Paschal discourse, "I will not leave you comfortless. I will come to you." He would come to them by the Person of the Holy Spirit, who is now the vice-regent of

Christ. When the Comforter comes He forms within the believer the living Christ. Paul prays for the saints at Ephesus, "to be strengthened with might by his Spirit in the inner man" (Eph. 3:16). To what purpose? "That Christ may dwell in your hearts by faith" (v. 17). This is the true secret of all practical scriptural holiness. We can never attain to true holiness by our own efforts and strivings, but only by surrendering to the Holy Spirit to form the indwelling Christ within.

*The Holy Spirit is not only the Agent for our sanctification, but He is also the Divine Helper in the ministry of intercession.* "Likewise the Spirit also helpeth our infirmities: for we know not what we should pray for as we ought: but the Spirit itself maketh intercession for us with groanings which cannot be uttered. And he that searcheth the hearts knoweth what is the mind of the Spirit, because he maketh intercession for the saints according to the will of God" (Rom. 8:26-27). Nowhere in the Christian life are we so baffled and beaten as when we seek to intercede on behalf of a languishing Church and a lost and dying world. How comforting it is to know that the heavenly Paraclete is the One who comes alongside to help us in this ministry by prompting and energizing our prayers.

*Not only in our Christian walk do we need the Holy Spirit, but also in our Christian service. All* true longings for the salvation of the lost are nothing less than the passion of Christ, reproduced in us by the power of the Spirit. It is only a Spirit-filled believer that can truly say: "I say the truth in Christ, I lie not, my conscience also bearing me witness in the Holy Ghost, That I have great heaviness and continual sorrow in my heart. For I could wish that myself were accursed from Christ for my brethren, my kinsmen according to the flesh" (Rom. 9:1-3). If we try to work up a passion for souls it will be only mere fleshly emotion. Only our mighty Intercessor can give us this burden.

Apart from the mighty enduement of power from the Spirit of Pentecost, all our Gospel service will be in vain. The natural, unregenerate man cannot comprehend "the things of the Spirit." His darkened mind can only be enlightened by the divine intervention of God, the Holy Ghost. He cannot be argued, fascinated, "bullied" or "enthused" into accepting Christ as his Saviour. It is not enough that we clearly expound the Gospel. It must be given in the demonstration and power of the Spirit and applied by Him. Paul wrote to the Thessalonians, "Our gospel came not unto you in word only, but also in power, and in the Holy Ghost" (1 Thess. 1:5). Peter reminded the sojourners of the dispersion that the Gospel had been preached to them "with the Holy Ghost sent down from heaven" (1 Pet. 1: 12). The sin that damns the soul is the rejection of Christ as Lord and Saviour. This sin of disbelieving on Christ is THE great sin, because it summarizes all other sins. Only the Holy Spirit can convict a lost soul of the sin of Christ-rejection and lead him to the foot of the Cross. As no person can be saved apart from the redemptive work of Christ, so also can no one be saved apart from the regenerating work of the Spirit. "And when He is come, He will reprove the world of sin, and of righteousness, and of judgment" (John 16:8). When asked on various occasions to speak at the preparatory meetings before the commencement of large evangelistic campaigns, I have seen the astonishment come over the faces of the Christian workers when I declared that there can be no revival among the saints and no regeneration among the unsaved apart from the work of the Holy Spirit. Many sincere, enthusiastic Christian workers have been deeply perturbed and even offended, and some have even gone so far as to accuse me of preaching a very discouraging doctrine when I insisted on this fact. Surely this is the first and foremost fact that every Christian worker must face in his service for God. I remember in one town being asked not to speak again to these preparatory groups, as I was only discouraging them in the work of the Lord. It is true that the Lord uses human instruments for the salvation of souls, but it is only when these instruments are yielded to His control that they can point guilty sinners to the Lamb of God.

> *No awful sense we find of sin,*
> *    The sinful life and sinful heart;*
> *No loathing of the plague within,*
> *    Until the Lord that feel impart;*
> *But when the Spirit of Truth is come*
> *A sinner trembles at his doom.*
>
> *Convinced and pierced through and through,*
> *    He thinks himself the sinner chief;*
> *And, conscious of his mighty woe,*
> *    Perceives at length his unbelief;*
> *Good creeds may stock his head around,*
> *    But in his heart no faith is found.*
>
> *No power his nature can afford*
> *    To change his heart, or purge his guilt;*
> *No help is found but in the Lord,*
> *    No, balm but in the blood He spilt;*
> *A ruined soul, condemned he stands,*
> *    And unto Jesus lifts his hands.*
>
> *—Berridge*

*Since there can be no awakening among believers and no regeneration of the lost apart from the supernatural workings of the Holy Ghost in and through the saints, it behoves every child of God to seek earnestly the enduement of power for his walk and witness.* We do not imply that it is God's will that all have the same empowering experience which George Whitefield or James Brainerd Taylor received, or that all shall be carried up the highest heavens as were Samuel Rutherford and Adelaide Newton, but we do insist that the anointing of the Spirit is to fit each one of us for the highest service in the work to which God has called us. I believe, from my study of the Word, and from a careful examination of the inner-experiences of holy men and women of God, that this mighty baptism is just as real an experience as that of regeneration itself. A careful reader of the Scriptures need not be told how closely the ceremony of anointing was related to all the important offices and ministries of the servant of Jehovah under the old Covenant.

The priest was anointed that he might be holy unto the Lord (Lev. 8:12).

The king was anointed that the Spirit of the Lord might rest upon him in power (1 Sam. 16:13).

The prophet was anointed that he might be the oracle of God to the people (1 Kings 19:16).

No servant of Jehovah was deemed qualified for his ministry without this holy sanctified touch laid upon him. Imagine, if you can, a priest attempting to minister before the Lord and daring to touch the holy things of the sanctuary without having first of all been sprinkled with the holy anointing oil! God was so jealous for the sanctity of those who had been anointed for service that the penalty of failing to wash the hands and feet when they ministered before the Lord was death (Exod. 30:19-21). What, then, but death in its most awful form must have been the penalty of such presumption as that which we have suggested? The holy anointing was the outward, visible sign of the impartation to the priests of those gifts and graces which qualified them for being the ministers of the Lord, the teachers, the guides, and the intercessors of the Lord's people.

Under the new economy every born-again, blood-washed child of God is a royal priest to minister before and for the Lord, and hence needs the anointing of the Spirit. The Church is a kingdom of priests, and each individual believer is a royal priest (Rev. 1:6; 1 Pet. 2:9).

*It is necessary for us to inquire concerning what preparation our Lord received to fully equip Him for His ministry here on earth.* I believe that he is our example in all things. "It is," says Pascal, "one of the great principles of Christianity that whatever happened to Jesus Christ on earth should come to pass in the souls and bodies of all that are His." One of the profound mysteries in the New Testament is that Christ needed to be anointed by the Spirit. Apart from the incarnation, no truth drives me to my knees in such adoration and worship as this amazing fact. The sinless, sovereign One, the One who always pleased the Father, the One to whom the Spirit was given without measure, must at His inauguration for His mediatorial work as Prophet, Priest and King receive a mighty enduement of power! As I arise from my knees with the awe of God upon my soul, I breathe reverently the following words:

"How amazing that my blessed Lord, my Kinsman Redeemer, needed this baptism."

If any Christian worker doubts that this is the true interpretation of the heavenly dove alighting upon the Son of God he needs only turn to the words of Peter for a full explanation: "How God anointed Jesus of Nazareth with the Holy Ghost and with power: who went about doing good, and healing all that were oppressed of the devil" (Acts 10:38). Oh,

162

dear child of God, if our Kinsman Redeemer could not begin His public ministry without this anointing, how can we be so presumptuous as to think that we can accomplish any work that can stand the scrutiny at Christ's judgment seat if we ignore this baptism! Too many are content to claim their share in Calvary who never go further and claim their share in the gift of Pentecost. They are content with the brazen altar, but never seek to enter into the "holiest of all." The upper room discourse of our Lord proves that it was His clear intention, through His ascension, to claim for His whole Church the same anointing of the Spirit as He Himself had received at His baptism. "The Spirit of the Lord is upon me, because He hath anointed me to preach" (Luke 4:18). The oil that anointed the head of our great High Priest was intended to fall upon us also, who are but as the hem of His garment.

Is there not a danger in these momentous days of the atomic and space age that we spend our time disputing about the power of the Spirit? In his day Dr. A. T. Pierson said that while theologians were contending as to what the baptism of the Spirit was, and were divided on the question as to whether it was proper to expect or even to ask for it in this dispensation, the incontrovertible fact was that men and women were both asking for and receiving a new and strange investment of power from on high, which somehow revolutionized their character, conduct, temper, and work. Said he, "We may best stop our discussion and go to praying." So deeply exercised was this precious man of God, that at the very height of his popularity he sat down and wrote his resignation from every committee on which he had been placed in order that he might give more time, himself, to this urgent need.

Too often even missionaries in the foreign mission field lapse into what we call a mere perfunctory routine of work which, among all Christian workers, is the most subtle of all snares.

Pilkington of Uganda declared that "But for the Spirit's special enduement that came upon me during a crisis in my life as a missionary, I would have been compelled to abandon the field and return home as a failure."

*The evangelical Church today is far removed from her Pentecostal prototype.* Hudson Taylor, at a Conference in New York in 1901, uttered these stirring words of challenge, out of a wealth of experience: "Today, the Holy Ghost is as truly available and as mighty in power as He was on the Day of Pentecost. But has the whole Church ever, since the days before Pentecost, put aside every other work and waited for Him for ten days, that the power might be manifested? Has there not been a source of failure here? We have given too much attention to methods and machinery and to human resources, and too little to the source of power, the Blessed Spirit." The message of the Acts of the Apostles is that the bare simplicities of the Gospel are the things that count. The glory of that dynamic Church was that transformed men proclaimed the Gospel with holy unction and certified it with holy lives. Our desperate need today is for a fresh enduement of power. This will be the authentic touch of God upon our lives.

The story is told of a noble woman in London city who after years of great usefulness in the service of the Lord was translated to glory. They carried her body into one of the greatest auditoriums that the city and the world might pay her honor. Lords and ladies and royalty came to pay tribute. The rich people of Britain and Europe came to look and weep. Then the poor people came pressing their way into the great building. The weeping thousands passed beside the sleeping woman. At last, a poor woman made her way down the aisle.

She had every mark of poverty as she carried a child in one arm and led another by the hand. When she reached the coffin, she put the baby on the floor, loosed the clasp of the older child's hand and then stooped to kiss the glass which covered the face, while the multitude sobbed in sympathy with her.

Who was she, sleeping in the coffin yonder? Why, none other than Mrs. Catherine Booth, the mother of the Salvation Army, one of the grandest women that God ever called into His service. The effectiveness of Catherine Booth's ministry is a true example of what the Holy Spirit can do in and through a human life, surrendered and obedient to His control.

Andrew Murray helpfully suggests the way into a fresh enduement of power by the following directions:

1.  I believe that there is a Pentecostal blessing to be received: the anointing of the Holy Spirit and enduement with power.

2.  I believe it is for me!

3.  I have never received it; or if I have received it once, I have lost it.

4.  I long and desire to secure it at all costs; and am prepared to surrender whatever hinders.

5.  I do now humbly and thankfully open my heart to receive all that I believe my Saviour is waiting to give; and even if there be no result in the emotion I will still believe that I have received, according to Mark 11:24.

Let us now go on our knees and pray reverently in the words of William Pennefather, the Church of England clergyman, whose ministry through the Mildmay Conference Movement lifted the evangelical Church of Great Britain to glorious heights some seventy years ago:

*Oh, Lord, with one accord*
*We gather round Thy Throne*

*To hear Thy Holy Word,*
 *To worship Thee alone.*
*Now send from heaven the Holy Ghost,*
*Be this another Pentecost!*

*We have no strength to meet*
 *The storms that round us lower;*
*Keep Thou our trembling feet*
 *In every trying hour;*
*More than victorious shall we be*
*If girded with Thy panoply.*

*Where is the mighty wind*
 *That shook the Holy Place,*
*That gladdened every mind*
 *And brightened every face?*
*Where are the cloven tongues of flame*
*That marked each follower of the Lamb?*

*There is no change in Thee,*
 *Lord God, the Holy Ghost!*
*Thy glorious majesty*
 *Is as at Pentecost.*
*Oh, may our loosened tongues proclaim*
*That Thou, our God, art still the same!*

*And may that living wave,*
 *Which issues from on high,*
*Whose golden waters lave*
 *Thy Throne eternally,*
*Flow down in power on us today,*
*That none may go unblest away!*

*Anoint us with Thy grace,*
 *To yield ourselves to Thee;*

*To run our daily race,*
    *With joy and energy,*
*Until we hear the Bridegroom say,*
*"Rise up, my love, and come away"*

# XIII

## Satan's Great Snare in Times of Revival

"The Spirit may be grieved by a spirit of boasting about the revival. Sometimes, as soon as revival commences, you will see it blazed out in the newspapers. Most commonly, this publicity will kill the revival."

—copied.

"It is a sign of immaturity and carnality for Christians to idolize the instruments of God."

—J.A.S.

The Message of this book would not be complete without our having left the reader with a warning concerning the reality of Satan's personality, activity, and subtlety. He is the archenemy of the Church, and the great antagonist of the Son of God. The Word of God abounds with warnings concerning his aggressive attacks against the Church of Jesus Christ. We find in these warnings that Satan's business is to deceive the saints by different stratagems. For example, Paul writes to the Corinthian believers that they should forgive one another, "lest Satan should get an advantage of us: for we are not ignorant of his devices" (2 Cor. 2 :11). He exhorts the Ephesian believers to "put on the whole armour of God, that ye may be able to stand against the wiles of the devil" (Eph. 6:11). The word "wiles" suggests a method or a cunning device of Satan which he uses to beguile the saints (see 2 Cor. 11:3).

One device of the devil is to get the believers proud of "their revival" and proud of their revival leaders. He suggests that it would be good and glorifying to God to publicize in a large way the wonders of the workings of His grace. Oftentimes, however, lurking at the back of this is self-exaltation, self-glory, and self-aggrandizement. It is well always to remember that the less we court publicity, when the Holy Spirit is doing His strange work, the purer and more lasting will be the results.

As we have mentioned in the previous chapter, the mighty workings of God's Holy Spirit is alone the efficient cause of revival. This truth, rightly understood, would rescue us from the folly and danger of attaching too much value to the use of the human instruments. We are too prone to overestimate, and even sometimes to idolize, these chosen vessels until God has to cast them aside that He may rescue us from such a dangerous delusion. We must never forget that no creature possesses or can possess any inherent value, and that all virtue, all power, and all glory belongs to God alone forever.

*Christ always comes in lowly guise, and always brings His cross with Him.* No one who has been used by God in revival ministry can ever forget the melting, the brokenness, and the humiliation before Him. Spontaneous, New Testament revivals begin in the secret of holy obscurity, with insignificant and broken instruments; instruments which have passed through a Gethsemane experience and have become worms before a great God. Great respect is certainly due to these blessed men and women of God, but we must be careful never to magnify them in an idolatrous way, as the world worships its film stars and sportsmen, and its heroes. When such idolatry takes place, the Holy Spirit is grieved and quenched and soon withdraws Himself from the revival movement.

"Let us make here three tabernacles, one for Thee, one for Moses and one for Elias!" cried Peter on the mount. While he was yet speaking these idolatrous words, a bright cloud obliterated the Christian leaders, and a voice from the most excellent glory announced sternly, "This is My Beloved Son."

When Bartimaeus asked what the commotion about him meant, the preachers did not answer, "We are passing by." True, it was their movements that arrested the blind man. He heard them. But when he asked what caused the commotion of the multitude, he was told, "Jesus of Nazareth passeth by."

Here is the secret of all true reports about revival: "JESUS OF NAZARETH PASSETH BY" (Luke 18:37).

> *What meaneth this eager, anxious throng?*
> *What moves with busy haste along?*
> *These wondrous gatherings day by day?*
> *What means the strong commotion, pray?*
> *In accents hushed, the throng reply:*
> *"JESUS OF NAZARETH PASSETH BY."*

It is said that the famous Russian masters, when painting the figures of Christ on their Greek Catholic Icons, would never sign their names to their work. When asked why, they replied, "How could we place our names beside the figure of the glorious Redeemer!"

How we all, leaders and people alike, need to pray constantly with the late Ruth Paxon, "O Lord, never let me ever touch Thy glory!"

Oh, beloved, it is only when revival is a matter of history that it may become the subject of applause. One writer has said, "If anything is to be said about revival, give only the plain and naked facts, just as they are, and let them pass for what they are worth."

"When Christians get proud of their 'great revival'," he continues, "it will cease. I mean those Christians who have been instrumental in promoting it. It is almost always the case in revival that a part of the Church proves too proud or too worldly to take any part in the work. They are determined to stand aloof and wait to see what it will come to. The pride of this part of the Church cannot stop the revival, for the revival never rested on them. They may fold their arms and do nothing but look out and find fault; and still the work may go on.

173

"But when the part of the Church that does the work begins to think what a great revival they have had, how they have labored and prayed, how bold and zealous they have been, and how much good they have done, then the work will be likely to decline. Perhaps it has been published in the papers as to what a great revival there has been in a certain church and how absorbed the members have been, so they think how high they will stand in the estimation of other churches all over the land, because they have had such a great revival. And so they get puffed up and vain, and they can no longer enjoy the presence of God. The Spirit withdraws from them and the revival ceases.

"The Spirit may be grieved by a spirit of boasting about the revival. Sometimes, as soon as a revival commences, you will see it blazed out in the newspapers. And most commonly this will kill the revival. There was a case in a neighboring state where revival commenced, and instantly there came out a letter from the pastor telling that he had a revival. I saw the letter, and I said to myself, 'That is the last that we shall hear of his revival.' And so it was. In a few days the work totally ceased. I could mention cases and places where persons have published such things as to puff up the church, and to make the people so proud that little more could be done for the revival.

"Some, under pretence of publishing things to the praise and glory of God, have published things that savoured so strongly of a disposition to exalt themselves —making their own agency stand out conspicuously—as were evidently calculated to make an unhappy impression. At a protracted meeting held in this church a year ago last fall there were five hundred hopefully converted, whose names and places of residence we knew. A considerable number of them joined this church. Many of them united with other churches. Nothing was said of this in the papers. I have several times been asked why we were so silent on this subject. *I could only reply that there was such a tendency to self-exaltation in the churches that I was afraid to publish anything on the subject."*

May God deliver us from immodest and sensational publicity! May we remember the solemn words of warning as found in the Old Testament scriptures: "And now, O ye priests, this commandment is for you. If ye will not hear, and if ye will not lay it to heart, to give glory unto My name, saith the Lord of Hosts, I will even send a curse upon you, and I will curse your blessings: yea, I have cursed them already, because ye do not lay it to heart" (Mal. 2:1, 2).

"I am the Lord: that is My name: and My glory will I not give to another" (Isa. 42:8).

# XIV
## An Urgent Appeal

"The day of Pentecost was a pattern day; all the days of this dispensation should have been like it, or should have exceeded it. But alas, the church has fallen down to the state in which it was before this blessing was bestowed, and it is necessary for us to ask Christ to begin over again."

—George Bowen

"God loves unity, and so He loves a united cry; a petition signed by more than one."

—Andrew Bonar

In 1724 Jonathan Edwards, in the midst of the mightiest awakening ever known on the North American continent, after much fasting and prayer, sent out his famous appeal for Christians of all lands to unite together to pray for a worldwide awakening and a return to primitive apostolic Christianity. A copy of this manifesto fell into the hands of William Carey, a modest English shoemaker, who was stirred to his deepest depths. He gathered a little group of believers together in his home to pray that God would do "a new thing" in their midst. Later, Carey republished Edwards' revival appeal, to which may be traced the mighty movements of the spirit which so characterized the nineteenth century, and also the worldwide missionary crusade, which was the most conspicuous feature of that period. William Carey became the father of modern missions.

Later still this same manifesto was used by God to change the spiritual life of Charles Finney, a converted young lawyer of New York state. Finney based all his revival-reasonings on this document. Jonathan Edwards' burden for revival caught fire in the heart of this young prophet, and once again revival fires began to burn in North America.

And later again, when President Finney was on a Mediterranean holiday for the recuperation of his health, the Holy Ghost so burdened him about the spiritual "slump" of the subnormal churches of North America that he began to prepare his now famous *Lectures on Revival*. These revival lectures have been read by Christian workers all over the world, and through their heart-warming messages revivals have broken out in many local churches and mission stations. This textbook has appeared in every leading language. Sometimes there has been printed ten simultaneous editions in the English language!

D. L. Moody and R. A. Torrey were greatly helped by Finney's lectures, so that once again the fire of God fell.

I often think that young Evan Roberts, when still in his teens, must have pored over the writings of Charles Finney far into the night. The burden of revival weighed down the spirit of this young man, so that whenever he appeared before the Lord's people he wept and pleaded with them to prepare their hearts for the coming of the Holy Spirit. From the Welsh revival sprung many fires which burned simultaneously in different parts of the world.

One of the most moving calls to revival fell from the lips of A. T. Pierson as he ministered to the world's greatest evangelical congregation during the illness of its pastor, Charles Spurgeon:

"In this church there has been for months past one of the sublimest spectacles that has ever created joy in heaven, or in the midst of men. On the second Sunday of last May your beloved pastor was suddenly attacked with disease, and for twenty-one weeks daily prayer was offered for him in this Tabernacle, at early morning and evening. In these meetings the whole church of God seemed to be represented. All united in heart supplication to the living God to spare a life that they accounted of more value than the precious gold of Ophir, the onyx, or the sapphire. I say with pathos and deep persuasion that since the time the disciples waited ten days before God in continuous prayer for Pentecost, or prayer was made 'without ceasing' of the Church of God for Peter when in prison, there has been no spectacle so sublime presented by the Church of God during all these eighteen centuries! And now, in the Name of God, I challenge this great Church of Jesus Christ to a spectacle more sublime than that which has greeted the eyes of angels or men. I *want to challenge you—and this is the solemn conclusion of this solemn appeal—to an unceasing and united prayer for a new coming of the Holy Ghost on the Church and on the world.*

"If this spectacle was sublime of all disciples of every name, uniting for the rescue of one beloved pastor from the jaws of death, how think you the heavenly hosts would thrill with delight, and even the heart of our Saviour, itself, if disciples of Jesus Christ of every name could be found represented in morning and evening meetings for prayer during six months to come, in this consecrated place, in an importunate, believing and anointed supplication that the greatest manifestation of the Holy Ghost since the days of Pentecost might come upon the Church of God in this apostate age. And this, that the world might soon hear the tidings of the Gospel, that, they might flash like electric lights from pole to pole, till every creature shall have learned the message of salvation, and that the Gospel shall have been preached as a witness to all nations, that the end might come, when the King in His glory shall once more descend to take His throne and wield His scepter over the world."

Now, to our closing challenge of this book. To all who yearn for a deep spiritual awakening I would suggest that in every congregation a prayer circle be formed without regards to number. The pastor should unite with himself any members in whom he discerns a peculiar degree of spiritual life and power and, without any publicity, or any direct effort to enlarge such a company, begin with these to lay hold on God.

181

The Holy Ghost, Himself, must add to the numbers and thus, quietly, and without observation, increase the little group under the blessing of the Lord. *It is essential that only prepared people, who are willing to pay the price for revival, join the prayer circle.*

*It is also essential that these prayer meetings be not hurried.* In my campaigns I often announce, "We are going to have a late prayer meeting. If you are nervous, or in a hurry to get home, kindly do not wait behind tonight, as the purpose of the meeting will be defeated. We want to have a quiet, unhurried waiting upon God." One must settle down in the Lord's presence before he can touch the Throne. It is in the stillness of the Holiest that the Father speaks. It is when we are quiet that the Holy Spirit prays through us. In order to have such definite prayer meetings for revival, Christians must be willing to sacrifice social pleasantries, and the comforts of life, including even sleep, and to lay aside everything that would hinder them in having these trysts with God.

*Another point which I would like to emphasize is that no one should publicly pray in such gatherings until God has given him the spirit of faith; otherwise the prayer of faith will be severely weakened.* I always tell the believers in large prayer meetings, "Kindly do not pray publicly until the Lord has given you the spirit of faith to believe that He is going to fulfil His Word." It is good sometimes for such believers to go aside together in mutual fellowship and cry to God until faith becomes their blessed portion. Faith grows upon the promises of God. Faith is grounded upon the Word of God. Thus it is necessary to study the Word and ask the Holy Spirit to seal it to your hearts. I have known on many occasions, when I was discouraged and downhearted, without any degree of faith that God would work in impossible situations, I was driven to the Book. After some hours in the Lord's presence, I got up from my knees with the Bible in my hands, singing;

> High are the cities that dare our assault;
>   Strong are the barriers that call us to halt!
> March we on fearless, and down they must fall,
>   Vanquished by faith in Him "far above all!"

*It is important that general prayers be omitted in gatherings to pray for revival.* Many meetings of such a nature are spoiled by some brother or sister praying general prayers around the world. Prayer, to be vital, must be definite. Ask the Holy Ghost to pray through you in vital intercession for the one definite purpose of the reviving of a subnormal church and the salvation of lost souls on their way to perdition.

*When the prayer meetings grow, under the blessing of the Lord, and larger numbers gather, it is necessary then to pray more for the restraining and constraining power of the Holy Spirit.* Many pastors are afraid to "throw open" the prayer meeting for united intercession because of the indefinite ramblings of some. One of the hardest things to acquire is the spirit of definite intercession. How few Christians will keep to the one theme of the meeting—revival! There is naturally a difference between a small group met together to pray and a large group—say of one thousand. In the small group the Holy Spirit sometimes burdens one believer to pray for half an hour, while in the large meeting this would be entirely out of place. When I have been conducting large prayer meetings I have asked the saints to make their prayers short and definite in order that a large number may take part. In a majority of cases four or five long prayers will kill the prayer meeting. In these large prayer meetings where sometimes several thousands have gathered, we have found that the prayers which are most effective are those which range from three to five minutes. Of course, one must be careful not to set a rigid standard in such a meeting, as the Holy Spirit is sovereign in His working, and sometimes overthrows our schedule.

Many times we have found it very profitable in a local church for different age groups to meet in different rooms for prayer. This is exceedingly helpful as it gives opportunity for some timid souls to break forth in intercession at the Mercy Seat. This helps to educate every soul in the assembly in the art of public prayer. It also gives more people an opportunity to take part.

It is preferable on many occasions for sisters to pray by themselves. In prayer meetings, when both sexes are present and the number is small, the conveners must be careful that at no time Satan be allowed an advantage. It is unwise, for instance, for sisters whose unconverted husbands have remained at home to meet for prayer with their brothers in the Lord whose unconverted wives are not present.

*Every pastor, the moment he accepts the pastorate of a church, should seek at the earliest possible moment to establish a circle of prayer during the twenty-four hours of each day, when at all times some saint will be on the "watch tower"* (Hab. 2:1). For over thirty years it has been our practice to carry on this twenty-four-hour chain of prayer in our meetings, with blessed results. I remember a church in Eastern Europe that built a special prayer tower, so that the members could carry on a cycle of prayer on the hour throughout the day and the night, as they looked down on the great needy city. In my whole life I never had such liberty in praying for any city as for that one. I seemed to understand with greater significance how Christ wept over Jerusalem.

*It is good also for every church to set aside one or two definite rooms for intercession which may not be used for any other purpose.* The setting apart of these rooms for the definite ministry of intercession somehow has a sobering effect upon the congregation.

If your local church is really sincere in its prayer for revival, I would suggest that you gather in the following manner:

1. Gather for prayer each Saturday night from eight o'clock till midnight.

2. On some week nights be prepared to pray as long as the Holy Spirit keeps you on your knees. Sometimes I have known that we missed a blessing from the Lord because some had not made preparation beforehand to remain longer.

3. On some occasions spend the entire night in prayer.

4. Each Lord's Day, gather for early morning prayer (the earlier the better, that the prayers will not be rushed) before the services of the day begin.

5. Have a prayer meeting prior to every Sunday evening Gospel service. I have found that it is almost impossible to preach the Gospel with holy unction if there has not been a red-hot prayer meeting beforehand. I always feel sorry and depressed when I find a church which does not weep for souls, at least before the Gospel service. Believers who come to this evening service without having spent time alone with God for blessing only lend to the coldness of the atmosphere.

6. Conduct a prayer meeting every weekday morning from 6-8 a.m. This may seem impractical, owing to the different working hours of the various members of the assembly. However, if the church will persevere, they will find a practical solution for this early morning meeting. Some can only attend for fifteen minutes before going to work, but we

have known many churches to be revolutionized through the early morning prayer meeting.

Believers who cannot attend these early morning prayer meetings should seek to attend meetings for prayer at other hours, so that the cycle of prayer may be retained. For example, those who work on night shifts can attend meetings in the afternoons. Mothers and homemakers can attend either forenoon or afternoon meetings. Those who work downtown can pray during the lunch hour.

*It is also necessary to conduct united prayer meetings, with all evangelical fundamental churches combining, from time to time.* How tragic it is to see a city or nation with several evangelical groups, crying to God for the same blessing, who are not united in their plea. Dr. Dale said, in his day, that even the sunrise over Rigi in Switzerland was not so glorious as seeing the light of the Gospel break forth in all its majesty in the hearts and lives of the thousands who attended Moody's meetings in Britain. May I say that there is no sight so glorious here on earth as that of some four or five thousand believers gathered together night after night for united intercession.

Andrew Bonar said, "God loves unity, and so He loves a united cry; a petition signed by more than one."

In these united meetings different local pastors, or the spiritual leaders in their churches, should preside on different occasions to lend unity to the cause. On other occasions some outside Bible teacher or evangelist should be invited, men who know the deep, mysterious workings of the Holy Spirit in revival. At these meetings a short message should be given from the Word of God relating to prayer and victorious Christian living. Short expositions of the revivals under Ezra, Josiah, Hezekiah, and Nehemiah, etc., are helpful. In all revival praying our faith must be based on the Word of God alone. Any movement towards revival that neglects the Word of God is bound to end in mere excitement.

*After relating how the revivals in the Bible were brought about, it is often very helpful to tell of the supernatural workings of God in the history of the Church.* These revival times are a source of great encouragement to the believers. "Sweet are the spots where Emmanuel has ever shown His glorious power in the conviction and conversion of sinners," said Samuel Rutherford.

One can understand the feelings of a Salvationist from the southern part of the U.S.A., on a pilgrimage to the city of London to visit the spot where William Booth commenced the work of the Salvation Army. After spending a hallowed time at Mile-End, he visited the Headquarters on Denmark Hill. There he gazed for a long time at the statue of the Founder. He was strangely moved. Reverently he knelt and sobbed out, "O Lord, do it again! O Lord, do it again!"

The father of William C. Burns, the minister at Kilsyth, encouraged himself in this same way. The subject of revival, as the great want of the times, had been for a long time in his mind and in the minds of the saints there. They could never forget what God did almost one hundred years before in the same parish. Into those sacred reminiscences and aspirations Mr. Burns entered most profoundly from the first day of his ministry in 1821. He labored unceasingly to keep alive, both in his own heart and the hearts of his people, the records of God's past dealings with His people. In 1822, the second year of his ministry, we find him, along with another congenial spirit, Dr. George Wright of Stirling, bending over the old records of the kirk sessions, bearing the dates 1742-1749 and with solemn interest deciphering the dim and fading lines that referred to the incidents of the work then in progress. Towards the close of the same year, and two successful summers, he preached directly and fully on the subject, taking for his text those singularly appropriate and impressive words in Micah 7:1, "Woe is me! for I am as when they have gathered the summer fruits, as the grapegleanings of the vintage: there is no cluster to eat: my soul desired the firstripe fruit," bringing the whole case of past attainment and subsequent declension before the people and calling upon them again to rise and seek the Lord.

Finally, on a Sunday afternoon, in August 1838, standing on the grave of his predecessor, Mr. Robe, on the anniversary of his death, he pleaded before a vast assembly of his people, in tones of unaccustomed earnestness which stirred the hearts of many in a manner never to be forgotten.

It was not very long after this that the heavens were rent and the whole parish was transformed like a garden of the Lord.

The pastor's son, William, in like manner, reminded the believers of the "high days of God." It was while he was calling to mind the great achievements of the Spirit at the Kirk at Shotts, in 1630, under the preaching of John Livingstone, that the whole congregation at his father's church were overwhelmed with the mighty power of God. "The power of the Lord's Spirit became so mighty upon their souls as to carry all before it like the rushing mighty wind at Pentecost." At the same time, in the pulpit of Murray McCheyne at Dundee, he read as a part of the pulpit exercises, Robe's Monthly Narratives of the mighty movements of the Holy Spirit in Scotland and other lands. These accounts so raised the tide of faith of the believers at St. Peter's that very soon they were in the midst of revival themselves!

*Let a record be kept of every definite petition laid before God.* We must not mock God. It is necessary from time to time in these prayer meetings to stand up and tell how God has answered prayer in the salvation of loved ones and other deliverances.

It is essential from time to time to have solemn definite acts of dedication, for entire surrender is indispensable to the prayer of faith.

May God guide us in beginning *today* a full preparation for His gracious visitation among us in reviving power, "For great is the Holy One of Israel in the midst of thee" (Isa. 12:6).